Political Parties

IN THE AMERICAN SYSTEM

 BASIC STUDIES IN POLITICS

Under the Editorship of

SHELDON S. WOLIN

University of California, Berkeley

FRANK J. SORAUF

Department of Political Science
University of Minnesota

Political

Parties

IN THE AMERICAN SYSTEM

LITTLE, BROWN
AND COMPANY
Boston

COPYRIGHT © 1964 BY LITTLE, BROWN & COMPANY (INC.)

LIBRARY OF CONGRESS CATALOG CARD NO. 64-13973

SIXTH PRINTING

Published simultaneously in Canada
by Little, Brown & Company (Canada) Limited

PRINTED IN THE UNITED STATES OF AMERICA

Foreword

LIKE SO MANY areas of human knowledge today, the study of politics and political institutions is undergoing significant changes. A quarter-century ago only a few voices challenged the prevailing consensus regarding the methods of political science, the choice of problems, and the relative weight assigned to the "factors" shaping political events, actions, and behavior. Since then a revolution of uncertain proportions has occurred, one that has been variously described as "the behavioral movement" or "social science." It has visibly altered the climate of political science and it has deeply affected the outlook of the political scientist. No longer does he believe that political science is a self-contained field. It has become second nature for him to utilize methods, concepts, and data drawn from a wide range of academic disciplines, such as sociology, psychology, and economics.

A marked self-consciousness about methods of inquiry characterizes much of the contemporary literature, whereas thirty years ago only a few political scientists were troubled by this concern. Today's political scientist is receptive to quantitative techniques, eager to emphasize measurement, prepared to devise complex classifications of empirical data, ready to experiment with abstract models, and engrossed with the intricacies of preparing questionnaires and organizing surveys of public opinion. These changes in method have also affected the outlook and the language of political science. Where his predecessors talked of "comparative government," he is apt to talk of "comparative political systems"; where they referred to "the process of government," he prefers to examine "the theory of decision-making"; and where they spoke simply of "political theory," he will, more often than not, insist on a distinction between "normative theory" and "empirical theory" and, depending on his candor or concerns, will assert that his main interest lies with the latter. It is perhaps inevitable that a moderate reaction should set in and that questions should be raised among political scientists about whether they have not gone too far and too fast. There is an uneasiness that some settled issues ought to be reopened; that important features of politics have been ignored; that questions of choice and value have to be restored to a central position; and that the wonder of politics has been lost amidst the preoccupation with abstractions, graphs, and mathematical tables.

In the light of these changes and uncertainties there is good reason for political scientists and political theorists to reflect on the changing nature of their field of study and to report to a less specialized, but no less interested, audience how political events, practices, and behavior appear to the contemporary political scientist; what way or ways of looking at these matters he has found most useful and fruitful; and what problems he considers to be genuine and important.

This series of books was designed for such a purpose. The authors do not attempt to provide simply a digest of relevant facts, but to offer reflections and systematic analyses of the more significant and interesting areas of political science and political theory. Some concentrate upon familiar topics, such as federalism and political parties, but they seek to suggest the theoretically interesting problems raised by these traditional themes. Other studies, such as those dealing with political theory and ideology, proceed on a more theoretical plane, but with the explicit intention of indicating their relevance to the empirical concerns of political science. The standard set for this volume by Professor Sorauf and for all the others is, I hope, within the best tradition of political science: the standard of reflective inquiry and informed analysis.

Political parties are, by almost any standard, among the truly novel features of modern political societies. Almost without exception contemporary political systems are peculiarly and preeminently "party regimes." This is true of totalitarian systems, like that of the Soviet Union, as it is of liberal democracies, such as the United States and Britain. Despite the universality of political parties and the admittedly fundamental part they play in political life, there is no "classic" work in the field comparable to Aristotle's comparative inquiry into constitutions, Machiavelli's essay on power politics, or de Tocqueville's analysis of democracy. It remains a field in search of a theory.

Although Professor Sorauf makes no pretense of filling this need, he does, I think, contribute in an important way to clarifying our understanding. In each of his chapters Professor Sorauf suggests concepts and hypotheses that he has found useful and illuminating in trying to comprehend the bewildering array of phenomena and relationships among phenomena that compose the universe of the political party. The temper of this book is experimental and receptive to many of the new methods of the political scientist. As an illustration, the concept of a "system" is utilized to suggest the way in which our two major parties operate, what functions they perform, how they interact with each other, and what their place is within the larger framework of political institutions and processes. The author experiments with the notion that the party employs a fairly definite pattern of "rewards" and "incentives" to promote its objectives, to maintain its competitive position with rivals, to discipline and satisfy its members, and to punish its rivals. At the same time, his study is attentive to the wider culture of which the party is a part, and he is careful to note the various ways in which American parties affect and are affected by their "environment." Above all, he makes abundantly clear that our parties not only contribute powerfully to the organization of our political life and to rendering its sprawling diversity more manageable, but also that the system of parties furnishes a vital mechanism whereby Americans make many crucial choices. Our parties are "screening devices" which sift candidates, programs, interests, passion, and ideologies, discarding what they deem unacceptable or even dangerous, and preserving what they believe will contribute to the success of the party. Whatever the reader's political preferences may be, he will come away from these pages with an appreciation of the conservative, stabilizing function performed by our party system, an appreciation that has been the despair of the reformer and the comfort of the satisfied.

Sheldon S. Wolin

UNIVERSITY OF CALIFORNIA, BERKELEY

Preface

My purposes in writing this short volume are two. I have sought, first of all, to suggest the perimeters of a full-range study of the political parties, one that will portray the party as an organization with structural characteristics and with a set of functions in the American political system. Second, I have tried to suggest the outlines of a theory of the political party by asking how the structures and roles of the party are determined and how the functioning party relates to the entire political process. As a more modest theoretical goal, I have tried by analysis and interpretation to explore the nature and operations of the American party system.

These goals suggest my feelings, indicated more fully in the Appendix, that the study of the American political parties has too often failed to present a total view of the political party. Too often a diverting fascination with Presidential elections or a study of the voting electorates has passed for a picture of the working political party. These goals also indicate my general feeling that anecdotal reporting and activism have too often taken political scientists from the task of generalizing and theorizing about the parties.

That view in turn reflects my feeling that the development of a theory of politics can best begin with theories of the middle range: that is, with theories explaining some process or institution within the total political system.

An interpretive treatise such as this one presents, to an unusual degree, the author's personal viewpoint. The judgments and interpretations are mine, but many of them have their roots in the ideas and writings of others. The scholars of the American parties have in various ways influenced my own understanding and ideas; my intellectual debt to the late V. O. Key is in this regard especially great. Similarly, my friends and colleagues, too many to number here, have helped me think through many of these problems, even though I have not been wise enough to accept all their suggestions. I am especially indebted to Nicholas A. Masters who has commented on this and other work of mine and who has shared his understanding of American politics with me. I am also grateful to my graduate seminars in political parties for hearing and challenging some of these ideas and to Rochelle Elliott, Caroline Wolf, and Herbert Weisberg for their work on various stages of the manuscript and proofs. Finally, my thanks go to Sheldon S. Wolin for his perceptive and valuable comments on this manuscript and its previous incarnation.

Frank J. Sorauf

UNIVERSITY OF MINNESOTA

Table of contents

1

2

3

Table of Contents

8

THE PARTY AND ITS
ENVIRONMENT, 135

9

TOWARD A THEORY OF
THE POLITICAL PARTY, 153

I

The political
party

As THERE are many roads to Rome and many
ways to skin a cat, there are also many ways to look at a political
party. One can see in the party a burning contemporary issue or
an ideological way of life, a bustling corps of political militants, a
casual alliance of indifferent or even cynical voters, or a compelling and charismatic leader. For political parties as complex and
multi-faceted as the major American parties, what they appear to
be may depend on the general political context of the moment, on
the particular part or activity of the party one views, or on the eye
of the beholder. Amid this variety and diversity the greatest problem is that of perceiving the political party in its entirety.

Indeed, the inclination is great to let the political party slip out
of focus entirely. It easily gets lost in the colorful and anecdotal
milieu of American politics. So intently may we follow the progress of Presidential campaigns in the United States, so fascinated
may we be by the clash of great personalities, by campaign charges
and counter-charges, that we lose sight of the role the parties play
in the nomination and election of Presidential candidates. Even if

we do not, we have seen only some parts of the American parties engaged in only one aspect of one of their functions — the contesting of elections.

A full-length portrait of the political party demands full assessment of the various organizations and personnel within the political party, as well as a complete picture of the functions the party performs in the political system. And so greatly do the political parties differ in structure and function that the generic concept of a "political party" may include the competitive electoral parties of Great Britain and the United States, the class-based parties of Latin American ruling elites, and the mass movements for independence in the new nations of Asia and Africa. Even within the United States "party" embraces the vital, electoral, major parties and esoteric splinter movements devoted to abolishing the income tax or alcoholic beverages.

PARTY AS FUNCTION AND ROLE

Unquestionably the most common function among the parties of the world's democracies — and the one that separates them most efficiently from other political organizations — is the mobilization of voters behind candidates for election. The major American parties, far more than most other parties, are dominated by the electing function. They are, indeed, great and overt conspiracies for the capture of public office. Yet within the entire American party system parties differ in the vigor and seriousness with which they pursue the electing function. For the major parties it is virtually the alpha and the omega. The cycle and seasons of their activity depend almost completely on the calendar of elections. But for the minor parties the election is little more than a convenient occasion for the achievement of some other political purpose. Not in their moments of wildest optimism can the Socialist Workers or Prohibitionists hope to capture the American Presidency or any of the governorships for which they contend. The ballot is for them a priceless, and low-priced, vehicle for publicizing and proselytizing their views.

Second only to the electing function is the party's role as a teacher — its function as a propagandist for political attitudes, ideas, and programs. Generally, the American parties have avoided the burden of promoting the vast world view that ideological parties such as the European Socialists assume. Their ambitions are more modest: a diffuse identification with the interests of labor or business or agriculture, for instance, or a platform with indistinct and often ambiguous policy stands. At a given time the American party may even adopt no more than a broad posture as the party of peace or prosperity.

The American parties — as all others — also perform the even more general educational role of political socialization. For its loyalists the party arranges the confusion of the political world. It teaches them how to view the political universe and its options. Its symbols offer them a point of reference in judging officeholders or in finding the "right" side in an issue or controversy. At the simplest level the parties help their clienteles to divide the political world into the statesmen and the scoundrels. For the more sophisticated follower the party relates a value or set of values — conservatism, racial equality, or national pride — to the policy or candidate alternatives he faces. Even though the American political parties share this function of organizing and directing political perceptions with the mass media and interest groups, they remain nonetheless a potent focus for organizing knowledge about American politics.

The parties of the democracies, third, assume in varying degrees the function of organizing the policy-making machinery of government. In the United States Congress and in state legislatures the basic unit of organization is the party caucus; from it flows the appointment of powerful presiding officers, committee chairmen, floor leaders, and steering committees. Performance of this function, of course, depends on the party's success as an electoral organization. The American party unable to win more than a handful of legislative seats and only an occasional executive post plays little or no part in organizing legislative and executive branches. Even though small bodies of voters may enable parties in multi-party systems to garner a share of parliamentary and cabinet power, policy-making power within the American political system depends on majorities.

The failure of the American parties to seize and use the policy-making power they so frantically pursue in their electing function has occasioned a fifteen-year debate within American political science. The academic advocates of "party responsibility" castigate the parties for failing to elect men who are loyal to an articulated program and who will enact the program into public policy once elected. More of that controversy later. It suffices to point out here that the failure of the American parties to assume this party function has become a subject of prickly controversy. Indeed, the major share of the history of the major American parties has been marked by an inversion of the usual party policy-making roles within government. Within the parliamentary systems of the Western democracies the parties have organized legislative majorities and blocs, at the same time as inviolable traditions of professional administrative services have kept them isolated from much of executive and administrative control. In the United States, though, the major parties have traditionally organized legislative chambers without using the party power for party-originated and party-identified policies. But they have, thanks to a long and largely honorable tradition of patronage, often been able to control the selection and operation of administrative services. Even as they yield the bulk of the patronage to merit-system appointees, they continue to control more top-level administrative appointments than do, say, the British political parties.

Finally, the political parties seem to be involved in a series of "non-political" functions. European parties, more frequently than the American, sponsor boy scout troops, social clubs for senior citizens, adult-education classes, and benevolent societies that offer group health and life insurance programs. In its fabled heyday the urban machine in America offered the new arrivals to the cities a range of services that made it, in contemporary terms, a combination of employment agency, legal aid society, social worker, domestic relations counselor, and community social center. And in the new style, urban "club" parties in the American cities and suburbs, the parties cater to the social and intellectual needs of a mobile, educated, ideological, often isolated upper middle class. The style may have changed from "beer all around" at the local tavern to martinis at the cocktail hour, but the parties continue to concern themselves with more than just campaigns and elections.

To refer to these functions as "non-political" is, of course, some what misleading. Although they may not seem to promise an immediate political payoff, the party hopes that in the long run they will create loyalties, obligations, and ties that will facilitate the successful performance of the other, more directly political tasks. The political party, in fact, exists solely for political purposes and performs only political functions. The other forms of political organization — the Church, the ethnic group, the informal community elite, the voluntary interest group such as a trade union or medical association — move freely from the non-political to the political function and quickly back again. Not so the political party. Its exclusively political character sets it apart from the other political organizations.

The emphasis a party places on one or two of these functions, and the style with which it carries them out, distinguishes it from its competitors and from the parties of other political systems. The balance of these functions that any party achieves, however, is not only a matter of making scarce energies and resources go around. Within many political systems the performance of one may be incompatible with the successful performance of another. In this regard American parties have long argued that they would compromise their success as electoral organizations were they to stress the development of programs and ideologies. They devote themselves entirely to the electing function and pay comparatively little attention to the business of promoting ideologies or organizing the powers of government. That electoral preoccupation distinguishes them not only from the minor parties in the United States but from the competitive parties of the other mature democracies as well.

The fact that political parties are exclusively political in function is no assurance that they monopolize the functions of contesting elections, proclaiming political programs and values, and organizing the machinery of government. The American parties, in fact, share the function of selecting and electing candidates with informal community elites in many localities. They also share with interest groups the maintenance of a system of responsibility in the American legislature. And in the function of spelling out political programs and alternatives they operate in uneasy competition with the mass media, educational institutions, and voluntary associations.

The classic urban machine in the United States came close to monopolizing these functions, but its palmier days are past. That the parties can no longer monopolize them suggests a changing role for them within the American political system.

THE PARTY AS STRUCTURE

The political party, though, is more than the sum of its fervid electoral campaigns, its advocacy of issues and programs, and its attempts to discipline officeholders. It is a stable organization, and it is a number of individuals and groups of individuals held together in a reasonably stable pattern of relationships by a multitude of purposes, incentives, and traditions.

There is an old and hoary image that pictures the political party as a series of concentric circles, like the ever-widening pattern of waves and ripples created by the pebble thrown into the pond. At the party's center of impact are the most active and most deeply committed partisans — the party cadre, the officialdom that maintains and leads the party organization. Then, in circular waves of decreasing vigor and impulse are arranged the party regulars and workers, the rank and file of party members, and finally the party's voters and identifiers.

The image is a simple and orderly one, although too precise for the reality of any political party, least of all the loosely organized American parties. Its shortcomings, however, suggest the problems in viewing any political party purely as an organization. For one thing, the metaphor of concentric circles suggests a regular, stable pattern of authority and activity within the party. Though some American parties may contain a series of groups differentiated by their activity and degree of involvement, others do not. It is a significant fact for countless local party organizations that their "active cadre" consists of no more than a county chairman and a few spiritless hangers-on. The lines of authority and the degrees of activity also may shift in time. The circles shrink, contract, and even collapse in the slack periods between elections.

Indeed, the image of the concentric circles assumes a party organization with a clear division of labor among its parts, a continuous pattern of activity through the year, and a clearly defined body of members and activists. The American political party matches none of these assumptions. None of the concentric circles within the American parties are clearly marked out. Because in many communities the American precinct committeeman is elected at an open primary, he may be either hostile to party leadership or largely uninterested in party operations. Informal leadership groups, coopted by a powerful party chairman or a party elite, frequently supplant the formal party organization. Nor is it easy to separate the party cadre and party workers from the personal followings of officeholders and candidates. Most local American parties are, especially around election time, an irrational and confusing amalgam of formal party officeholders, informal party leadership groups, and the personal followings of candidates. And since in the United States card-carrying party membership is not widespread — and is, indeed, even faintly suspect — the circle of formal membership does not even exist in many American parties.

The most vexing problem with the analysis of the concentric-circle model concerns the question of whether or not, in searching for the party as an organization, we follow the circles to infinity. The party officials, the party actives, and even the party members, we may call the party "organization." Popular usage in the United States does. Beyond the "organization" are the party's voters, its supporters, and its "identifiers." Their ties of loyalty and activity are often most tenuous. These identifiers, the passive "fellow travellers" of the party, may share the party goals or ally themselves loosely with its prospects and fortunes. In those Western countries systematically furrowed by the opinion pollers, they are the men and women who respond to questions such as: "Do you think it will make a good deal of difference to the country whether the Democrats or the Republicans win the elections this November, or that it won't make much difference which side wins?" or "In politics, do you consider yourself a Democrat or a Republican or a member of some other party?" With the identifiers on the outer peripheries of the party are the partisans who vote (with some regularity) for the candidates of the party. The identifiers and the voters overlap considerably. But even though their support is crucial to the party's success, they hardly share the stable relationships and authority of the party structure. In this sense the "party-in-the-electorate" is less an organization than a reaction to a symbol and a tradition.

The political party as an organization consists, however, of much more than a series of concentric circles or superimposed layers of organization. It is a hierarchy of parties, from local unit to national party, through which the parties achieve a geographical division of effort. In federal systems such as that in the United States the parties' decentralized internal relations parallel and reflect the decentralization of the political system. The multitude of delicate relationships between and among the party units suggest another important aspect of party organization. So do the decision-making processes by which the party selects leaders and candidates, makes and enforces policy decisions, and allocates effort and responsibility within the party. Furthermore, the political party may be approached organizationally as a system of incentives and goals that bind the partisans together and spur them to action.

Viewed as systems of power and authority, the political parties exhibit sharply contrasting organizational features. They run from the centralized, militant, and disciplined structures of the European Socialist and Communist parties to the decentralized, virtually autonomous, cadre organizations of the American major parties. Even within American local party organizations the range extends from the tough, almost hyperactive urban machine to the immobile, chaotic, disorganized parties of many rural areas, from the traditional party of the exclusive circle of workers to the new, membership, club types of parties. Often, indeed, the variations in party organization from time to time and place to place within one party are more interesting and instructive than the differences among a number of parties.

PARTY IN THE DEMOCRATIC SYSTEM

When we talked earlier of the functions the parties perform, we referred only to their immediate ones: the manifest functions. These are the tasks party leadership sets out consciously to perform and on the performance of which the party's immediate success or failure depends. In performing them the parties also perform remoter, indirect, "latent" functions. It is as if, by performing immediate functions A, B, and C, the party fortuitously performs also the useful functions X, Y, and Z. For example, as the party goes about the immediate tasks of nominating and electing candidates for office, it is at the same time recruiting political leadership. Indeed, as it selects candidates from its own cadre of active workers, it may also be functioning as a training school for political leaders. To put the matter in another way, the party performs certain tasks (the manifest ones) that ensure its own successful functioning, at the same time performing others (the latent ones) that contribute to the functioning of the entire political system.

Only in the party's latent functions is the relationship between it and the political system clear. The chief manifest functions the parties perform — the nomination and election of candidates, the support of issues and ideology, and the organization of government power — can be and are performed by the parties of totalitarian political systems as well as by the democratic parties. But the ways in which the parties choose, and are permitted, to perform them determine the sharply different latent consequences. When one begins to list the latent functions of the American and British parties it soon becomes clear that he is talking of parties operating in and forming an integral part of democratic political systems. And a comparison of those of the British and American parties with those of the parties of the new nations of Asia and Africa soon indicates the different party contributions to differing varieties of democracy. The dominant, single parties of some of the new nations clearly function within a Rousseauist democracy of solidarity and national purpose rather than in the pluralist, competitive democracy of the United States.

The parties of the democracies, both by supporting candidates for office and by representing interests and issues, simplify the choices confronting the voters. By reducing the contestants for public office and the options of public policy to two, three, or even a handful, the party simplifies — doubtless oversimplifies — the political choices into terms the average citizen can grasp. The stability and continuity of the party symbols, heroes, and slogans gives him fixed points of political reference, thus maintaining the simplicity of choices over the years. In the various ways in which

the parties nominate and elect they play a crucial role in the
recruitment of political leadership. Especially in those vigorous
American party organizations in which the office-seeker must
work his way tortuously up the party hierarchy, the party is the
gateway through which the ambitious must pass and be passed.
Finally, by organizing individuals, interests, and groups into
broader political aggregates, the parties mediate and compromise
the clash of political interests and ideologies.

In all of these ways the tie between the political party and the
democratic regime is clear. The parties facilitate the popular participation, the representation of interests, and the presentation of
alternatives on which the processes of democracy depend. They
augment the representational processes of the democratic system
by providing an organizational link between political man and the
institutions of government beyond the one provided by the formal
election machinery. They organize the loyal opposition and the
democratic dialogue of the "ins" and "outs." So closely are our
concepts of party tied, not only to democracy, but also to Western democracy, that they have limited relevance to the parties of
national independence and development in the newer nations.
Most Americans find it difficult to think of the single, dominant
parties of these nations as "genuine" political parties. Much less
than the parties of the older democracies do they propose alternative candidates and programs, but to a far greater extent, they do
carry out the more general functions of political education, socialization, and communication.

The relationship between the party and the democratic regime,
though, is neither fixed nor beyond challenge. Much of the scholarly criticism of the parties of the United States grows out of the
deep-seated suspicion that the American parties fail to carry their
share of the democratic burdens. The American parties, their critics charge, fail in their obligation to augment — and give meaning
to — the democratic system of representation and policy making.
The difficulty lies in the haphazard and sporadic way in which
they perform the manifest functions of contesting elections, stating
programs, and organizing the machinery of government. Their
critics would have the parties pursue the three functions more
vigorously and systematically so that they might provide the in-

formation, the choices, and the promise of action the citizen needs for his democratic decisions to be meaningful. In this sense the dispute over "party responsibility" is in reality a dispute over the kind of democracy we are to have. Those who argue for it maintain simply that the democracy of a direct individual-to-government relationship depends for success on the intermediate organizing services of a political party.

The American political party also acts in another sense on behalf of majoritarian democracy. It has increasingly become the instrument through which massive, popular majorities exert their influence within the political system. By organizing sheer numbers it offsets the advantages of wealth, expertise, status, and access that minorities may enjoy. As William Chambers has put it:

> . . . parties may serve as democratic counterforces to advantages in power. Only through time can they affect the economic and social conditions of "the poor and middling class." They can exert a more immediate impact on other factors of power potential, however, if certain minimal conditions obtain in the populace, such as awareness of interests, some propensity for political participation or initiative, and receptivity to association or organization. Parties may offer leaders and leadership; and through their structure they may diffuse knowledge and skill in political tasks, stir the sense of political consciousness and efficacy, promote cohesion in their followings, and develop tools of association or organization. They may also counteract the weakness of "divisions" among the "common people," in Melancthon Smith's words, by drawing them together into popular partisan combinations. Thus they may call forth and mobilize the latent strength of numbers.

Especially in this century the political party, joined increasingly with strong and vigorous executive leadership, has helped create a truly popular, mass democracy.

The relationship between the democratic political system and its political parties is a complex one, full of reciprocal influences. The party is to a great extent an essential instrument, a necessary condition or ingredient of democracy as we know it. But though it may be in this sense a prerequisite of democracy, it also is democracy's child. The rise of the political party in the Western democracies parallels the rise of demands for greater popular participation in public affairs. The first enduring party in the United States, the Jeffersonian Republicans, extended its support to the grass roots to meet the growing democracy there. Its early competitor, the Federalist party, failed at least in part because its elitist, antidemocratic values prevented it from building the loyalties and following it increasingly needed. It could neither serve nor survive as a party of notables committed to notions of a closed, governing elite. Later the mass, presidential politics of the Jacksonians built largely on a rapidly expanding electorate and an expanding democratic participation. Even the early urban machine of the late 19th century must be understood in part as an attempt on the part of the newcomers to the cities to wrest their governance from old elites and aristocratic families.

In England during the 19th century the Tories and Whigs, at that time not much more than legislative caucuses, were forced by the expansion of the electorate to send out organizers to set up constituency political parties in order to maintain their strength in Parliament. The origin of the modern parties in Britain dates directly to the expansion of the suffrage in the great Reform Acts of 1832 and 1867. Later expansions in the European electorates to include the new industrial workers found expression in the new, mass-membership workers' parties. The expansion of the democratic suffrage not only created the need for the party to aid in the organization of democratic consensus; it also meant that no man or group could any longer maintain itself in political power apart from great aggregates of popular approval and support.

TOWARD A DEFINITION OF PARTY

Of all our major political institutions the political parties have most developed in a spirit of improvisation and jerry-building. The American constitution mentions them not at all, nor has the Congress tried to define their structure or activities. They have been left to develop in response both to diverse local political styles and needs and to varying state legislation. To a large extent party is as party does. The resulting diversity complicates the problem of defining the political party broadly enough to encompass all the American parties. That problem reaches staggering proportions when one broadens the task to include the parties of all the democracies.

Popular usage often confuses the partisan with the political. All party activity is political, but not all political activity is partisan. The concept of politics suggests that complex of individual and group attempts to exert influence on the selection of public officials and on the making of public policy. The debate over what is and is not political — and over where the boundaries of politics run — is probably the oldest unsettled and unsettling issue in political science, but this is hardly the place to measure again the terrain of that battlefield. There is, however, a consensus that it is in this political process that the parties perform their tasks. They may dominate it, but they never completely monopolize it. In fact, they may yield the major role to other political organizations in some sectors of the political process. One often finds interest groups playing roles of greater influence than the parties in the passage of bills in the United States Congress.

The chief definitional problem, then, rests in distinguishing the political party from other organizations, organizers, and intermediaries in the political process. It has been common to belabor the differences between the party and the interest group, or "pressure group," if one prefers a less neutral term. But the party must also be distinguished from the informal elites of the community, the personal clique, the fluid and restless faction, and the basically non-political group — a corporation or a church, for instance — engaged in sometime political activity. They too, with the political party, perform organizing and coalescing functions in the political process.

With these considerations in mind, the political party may be defined as an agency for the organization of political power characterized by exclusively political functions, by a stable structure and inclusive membership, and by the ability to dominate the contesting of elections.

In function the political party limits itself to the political. Other political organizations — the interest group, the community elite, the newspaper, for instance — have non-political lives and functions. The American Medical Association devotes only part of its energies to protecting its interests through political action. Not so the political party. It arises and exists solely as a response to the problems of organizing the political process. One of its greatest continuing problems, indeed, is that of minimizing the political roles and influence of its non-party competitors.

Among those political functions the one the parties come the closest to monopolizing is the electing function. So successful have the parties been here, aided by state laws that define the parties solely according to their electing roles, that the temptation is great to define them in that way. The parties, however, execute the electing functions in many ways and with many degrees of seriousness and success. Though that may be their distinguishing function, it need not be their chief one. A definition of party resting on the elective role risks that confusion. It may also overlook the fact that non-party organizations increasingly — especially in the non-partisan elections of the United States — recruit and support candidates for office. But, making all allowances for these reservations, the party remains the electoral organizer par excellence in the democracies.

A stable and inclusive organization also marks the political party. It is *stable* in that it persists beyond the single cause or the single election. It acquires traditions, clienteles, and ideologies that live on beyond the fleeting policy issue or mortal man. Given this stability it may become a symbol, a focus of loyalty, and a point of orientation for its public. The party is *inclusive* in the sense that it appeals for and welcomes new adherents to its goals, its candidates, and its symbols. The party expands willingly, seeking constantly to broaden and solidify its base of support. And, as easy as it is to overlook it, the political party is an organization, with the ordered internal relationships and the division of labor that the word "organization" implies.

By these criteria the political party is more purely political than the voluntary organization or elite turned to politics for a passing issue. Its range of political activities extends more regularly to the elective role than do those of interest groups. Furthermore, it develops a public life and existence of greater duration and impersonality than does the faction, the *ad hoc* political organization, or the political clique. And it develops more stable and more elaborately differentiated organizations than those of any of its competitors.

This definition of a political party is nothing if it is not modest. It merely describes the parties, especially those of the United States, as they are, not as they "ought to be." It is intended to meet what is probably the greatest test of a definition of political party — the two major American parties. They are so atypical of the democratic parties in so many ways that one generalizes from their experience only at the greatest peril. Only the broadest definitional categories will embrace them along with the parties of the Western democracies and the developing nations.

2

Parties
in systems

THE CONVENTIONAL image of the party system envisions a political marketplace in which the parties compete for the loyalties and favor of the political consumer. Basically the single criterion for categorizing party systems has been that of their competitiveness in bidding for voter support. The one-party, two-party, and multi-party designations indicate the number of competitive (major) parties in the system. The non-competitive, minor parties — which, of course, do not count in defining the system — are those which go through the motions of electoral competition without any real prospects of success.

Although the general criterion for defining party systems is clear, it is less clear what we mean by competitiveness. In a general sense the political party is competitive if it has a genuine chance of winning elective office and competing for a share of the policy-making power of government. The competitive parties in the system are those which control the selection of the elected and politically responsible officeholders. But is the party competitive at 25 per cent of the vote? Or at 35 or 40 per cent? The party consistently polling 40 to 45 per cent of the vote in a two-party system is not, in the narrow sense, more competitive than the party that struggles along at 20 or 25 per cent of the two-party vote. It does, however, exert a greater impact and check on the campaigns, candidates, and policies of the winning party, even though it never wins an election. And if it has consistently flirted with the 45 per cent marks in the past, its future possibilities cannot be lightly dismissed. Competitiveness is a matter of probability of victory, and probabilities depend largely on past performance.

Furthermore, a concept of competitiveness must have dimensions of time and space. One serious defeat does not make a minor party of the loser, but three or five or seven may. A party's competitiveness, moreover, may not be evenly spread over the geographical extent of a political system. Consider the party that wins several parliamentary seats, thanks to a regional concentration of its support, while winning less than 10 per cent of the national legislative vote. Is it more or less competitive than the party that gains no seats while winning 15 to 20 per cent of the total vote? Or consider the possibility that in federal systems parties may be competitive within the regional governments but not nationally. Several parties compete with the Congress party in some of the Indian states, but none do nationally. American third parties such as the Populists, the Progressives, and the Socialists have been locally competitive, although they never achieved major party status nationally.

The resurgence of the British Liberals in the 1960's illustrates most of these problems in determining competitiveness. As of 1963 they held less than 2 per cent of the 630 seats in the House of Commons, and no pundits gave them any real chance of winning more than a modest bloc of parliamentary seats in the foreseeable future. And yet the party was mustering sufficient support to win an occasional by-election and to hold a balance of power in many others. Some observers saw the possibility that in a closely fought general election it might prevent both the Conservatives and the Laborites from winning a clear majority of seats. Though the Liberal party shows little potential for a stunning national victory, it may well have a very audible voice in determining the fortunes of the other two parties. Query: do the Liberals meet the

canons of competitiveness? Query again: as of 1963 has Great
Britain a two-party or a three-party system?

To all of these definitional queries there are no easy answers. In
many ways we have come no further than British electoral law,
which considers all candidates polling less than one-eighth of the
total vote to be frivolous and non-competitive and, therefore, not
entitled to a refund of their £150 electoral deposit. Even if we
do work out some standards for determining the probability of
electoral victory, we should probably extend the concept of competitiveness to include those parties which despite gloomy prospects for victory can materially affect the competitive positions
of the major parties. By that standard one would have to say that
Britain has at least temporarily entered a period of three-party
competition. Finally, there is also a strong case for tailoring one's
standard of competitiveness to fit the role of the parties in the political system. The British parties, obliged to build governing
majorities in the parliamentary system, compete for a share of
legislative and cabinet power. The American parties, on the other
hand, compete to a far greater degree for the elective office per se.
A party winning 5 per cent of the legislative seats in the House of
Commons or any parliamentary system is more likely to be competitive than one that wins the same percentage in the American
House of Representatives.

This overriding criterion of competitiveness, on which we erect
our categories of party systems, reflects a functional approach. In
particular, it reflects an almost compulsive concern with the electing function. It measures only the party's ability to win elections,
ignoring even the quality of the competition. It makes no distinction between the passive winning party and the party that ham-
mers its electoral triumphs out of hard, aggressive organizational
work. It makes no allowance for the losing party that, even though
it loses regularly, forces the majority party to broaden its appeal
or to adopt more appealing candidates. Nor does it evaluate the
party's performance of its other functions — in raising issues or
criticizing the exercise of governmental power.

The categorization of party systems is a monistic one built on
the single, often poorly defined dimension of electoral competition. There is, however, no intrinsic or even profound reason why

it must be so. We might, for instance, develop a set of categories that would describe the allocation of a number of political functions among the parties of a system. Or we might assess the parties by structure as well as by function, recognizing at least the difference between cadre and mass-membership parties. If the parties do indeed perform more than the electing function, then they interact and compete in terms of functions beyond that of contesting [electio]ns. The very concept of "system" demands the inclusion of [the] relationships and divisions of effort among the parties.

[L]imited a typology of party systems as this may be for the [Western party systems, it is dramatically less adequate for [pa]rties of the developing democracies. Electoral competitive-[ness as] a measure of party systems assumes that the major bulk of [co]nflict and competition in a democracy will be channelled [into in]ter-party competition. The democratic politics of the newer [state]s involve the problems of political integration and solidarity [more] than the competitive dialogue of differences and alterna-[tives. C]Often a single party dominates the elections of the country, [holdin]g within itself most of the viable political alternatives. Po-[litical] competition, if it exists at all, may be intra-party rather than [inter-p]arty in nature, or may be between the party and non-party [group]s such as traditional elites and ethnic organizations.

[Des]pite its weaknesses, the competitive standard for the party [system] measures the American party system more fairly than it [does t]hose of most of the other democracies. For the American parties the electoral function is indeed the cardinal party function. The business of ideology and governmental power is less important to them than to other parties. The American major parties, by piecing together constantly shifting majorities of fickle voters, best approximate the kind of inter-party competitiveness that the definition of "party system" basically depends on.

THE AMERICAN PARTY SYSTEM

Among the usual three categories of party system — the one-party, two-party, and multi-party — the American two-party system stands a somewhat lonely watch between the multi-party systems of the Western democracies and the tendency to one-party systems in the new nations of Asia and Africa. It is true that Uruguay has had two stable contesting parties for 100 years, but one of them had won no national elections until the late 1950's. Colombia, too, has depended on two competitive parties, but their successes and failures have often been achieved or augmented by extra-party and extra-legal means of winning governmental power. Indeed, only the party systems of the United States and Great Britain appear to meet the classic two-party criteria, and at that, the British system has veered to tri-partyism at least twice in this century.

The competitive major parties in a system such as the American are of necessity majority parties. The task of winning elections is an exercise in building majorities, and it dictates the necessity for a broad, inclusive appeal to the electorate. The American party must find within itself room for the tenant farmer and the big-city businessman, for the traditional Southerner and the mobile Californian, for the young intellectual and the retired trade unionist. Inevitably, it inclines toward loose, diverse, non-dogmatic groupings held together by traditional loyalties, a search for immediate rewards, and the momentary appeal of candidates. So inclusive may it be that it can compromise internal differences of goal and interest only at the price of a nebulous moderation in its program.

Not all two-party systems fall into a single, unvarying mold. They all produce loose, inclusive, majoritarian parties, but significant differences may distinguish them. The British two-party system has provided a greater ideological distinction between the two major parties than has the American. It has, furthermore, provided more cohesive legislative majorities than has the American system. The two-party systems of the two countries have, in other words, developed special characteristics that reflect the differing governmental systems of the two countries, differing sets of political cultures and traditions, and the differing population characteristics of their voters. Their similarities are best highlighted not in comparing one with the other, but by contrasting them with the single- and multi-party systems.

There is one useful distinction to be made among the two-party systems, though. In the American and British systems the major parties cut across all groups in the society "horizontally," each party taking or willing to take some of each into its coalition.

Though the Republicans and Democrats in the United States do not share equally the support of farmers, organized labor, businessmen, Catholics, Protestants, and Jews — to mention only a few groups — each does enlist the loyalty of significant numbers of all of them. Neither party ignores or writes off the political interests and aspirations of any major group. Because they are truly national and inclusive parties, cutting across and representing most major groups in the society, one may say they form a horizontally divided two-party system. Their inclusiveness, of course, does not result solely from their preferences. Because individuals in the society have many conflicting and overlapping group associations and loyalties, and because they do not all accept the same issue or group membership as the chief or overriding one, the parties could not organize them along a single axis even if they were so inclined. Because the two parties do divide the electorate horizontally, neither party's loyalists are safe from the competitive raids of the other.

By contrast, a two-party system such as South Africa's cuts the community sharply, and vertically, into two groups. The Nationalist party draws largely on Afrikaner, *apartheid* support, and the Union party represents the English-speaking population and its less-restrictive racial policies. Although differences between the two parties are no longer as sharply drawn as they were, they still glare at each other over the great divide of a single issue, *apartheid*, and its related ethnic loyalties. Dogmatism and commitment replace compromise and free bidding for voter support. The vertical two-party system can stage only a token or arrested competition. Open competition for movable voters is no longer possible in a society in which a single issue or loyalty so totally absorbs and subordinates all other political interests.

The American party system, viewed nationally, has not for almost a century and a half slipped into one-partyism. Even during the years of the Rooseveltian landslides of the 1930's the Republicans contested for the Presidency with great hope of victory. The *Literary Digest*'s prediction in late October of 1936 that Alf Landon would win 57 per cent of the two-party popular vote in the coming Presidential election struck very few contemporaries as outrageous or preposterous. Nor has the American party system experienced multi-partyism since the Civil War. The history of Presidential elections since then is strewn with the shattered hopes of third-party bids — the failure in 1924 of the La Follette Progressives to carry more than the candidate's home state, the failure of the Socialists to draw even a million voters in the depression-dominated election of 1932, the inability of Henry Wallace to carry a single state in his 1948 challenge to American foreign policy.

Yet as all party systems do, the American has within it party sub-systems that bear striking similarities to the one-party and multi-party systems of other political systems. Within federal systems the existence of semi-autonomous regional governments offers the parties additional sets of electoral prizes for which they can compete. Given differing local traditions and special local populations, the American states have seen the development of special one-party systems. For longer than most Republicans care to remember, the South has been a Democratic one-party area. The Republicans until very recently enjoyed a similar hegemony in parts of New England and the Middle West. A recent and careful classification of the state party systems in the United States, based on the years 1914 to 1954, found that only a few more than half (26 of 48) met standards of competitiveness in state-wide races. Ten Southern states, all Democratic, were designated one-party states, and another 12 (eight Republican and four Democratic) were classified as modified one-party states. These 22 state one-party systems were, of course, dominated by Democratic strength in the Southern and border states and by Republican strength in New England and the prairie states.

Strangely, Americans view their own one-party systems far more generously than they do those of other parts of the world. But single-party systems within democracies, such as the Congress Party in India or the Mexican Party of Revolutionary Institutions (P.R.I.), bear much in common with the Democratic party of the American solid South. Regardless of location, homogeneity is the hallmark of the one-party system. It reflects the single, overriding tradition, goal, or ideology, or the single dominating social group or interest. In the case of the one-party systems of the developing areas, the dominant party grew out of the movement for independence and now represents the new national goals. It speaks for the new nationalism, the push for national economic development, and the new dignity of independence and self-government. That unity over national traditions and the national mission carries them, for the moment at least, over the incipient conflicts of increasingly plural societies. The Democratic party of the American South has, similarly, been a product of that region's resistance during Reconstruction. During those years the Republican party became synonymous with Negro rule and the enforcing power of the national government. The Democrats were, not unlike the new parties of Asia and Africa, identified with autonomy, self-government, and a deeply felt way of life.

Underlying the single competitive party also may be the dominant class or interest. In the case of the American South this homogeneity has been achieved in part by a restrictive suffrage that creates an artificially homogeneous electorate in a somewhat more diversified society. In a federal system the one-party subsystems occur most frequently because of small pockets of a unified and dominant local interest. The lines of division in the competitive, heterogeneous national party system divide the voters of the country along broad interest lines, but those interests are distributed unevenly over the country. Hence the interests of American agriculture in the Middle West dominated the politics of the prairie states for many years and furnished the basis for a one-party system in many of those states. Once the dominant tradition or interest embeds itself in a dominant political party it tends to perpetuate itself. One-party rule depresses political interest and awareness at best, and at worst it promotes a solidarity behind community goals that identifies dissent with rejection of the favored social values.

Inevitably the single party must embrace an enormous range of political and non-political diversity, even despite the unities of great traditions and overriding interests. In the American context the unity of the single major party has often been broken by factionalism within the dominant party. The dissent and diversity within the single party may produce a competition among factions, but generally it is a pale and poor substitute for party competition. It offers the voters no continuity of programs or leadership, no continuity even of the party traditions and symbols. Only the persons and followings of dramatic, flamboyant leaders afford any focus around which the factions will cohere. In its most exaggerated form that personalism produces the wildly extravagant personalities and demagogues that long marked the Southern political style. Within these shifting, almost kaleidoscopic, factions cohesion is maintained, not by the usual loyalties to party, but by personal friendship, magnetic leadership, and the tangible rewards of favors and patronage. Since only the extraordinary political leader can dominate the faction of statewide scope, these factions more frequently are coalitions of personal followings, drawing together the power of courthouse bosses and barons in a grand exchange of quid pro quos. In such a free-wheeling combination and recombination of coalitions one often finds old enemies in new embraces of convenience, for the lines dividing factions are both less distinct and less permanent than those dividing political parties.

Ultimately this factionalism in the single competitive party may reach a state of extensive formality and stability. In a number of Southern states the Democratic party factions, organized around the figures and dynasties of men like the Byrds and the Longs, represent regional and economic interests, much in the same way as the formal "sectors" of the Mexican P.R.I. represent economic interests and compete among themselves for the party's all-powerful nominations. Even where the factions achieve this stability, and especially where they don't, they find it difficult to assume the role of the party. Factional competition is at best a poor surrogate for party competition. The lack of continuity and stability in the factions permits little systematic organization of a responsible opposition, and a system so given to personalism and the magnetism of the extroverted leader finds it difficult to recruit new political leadership with any care or system. That, one might note, remains a problem not only in the American one-party areas, but also in the younger one-party systems such as those in India and Ghana. And even more than the usual American party, the single party finds it difficult to state issues and carry out programs. Its inclination is to an issueless politics of immediate reward.

In the one-party states of the American South, V. O. Key points out, the single parties and their factions even carry out the electing function less effectively:

> In a two-party state a nominee for governor, say, has a ready-made machine of sorts; he has a following among the voters that will support him, as the nominee of the party, through thick and thin. He has only to strengthen an organization that already exists, to enlarge the loyal party following by the recruitment of the independent and wavering vote. In a one-party state, such as Alabama, the building of a faction by a state-wide leader must start almost at the bottom, and an especially heavy reliance has to be placed on the dispensation of favors, on the promise of favors, and on the appeal of individual personality.

What has been true of the South has, happily, not been completely true of the rest of the country. In the one-party states of the North and West the second party, supported by local and city triumphs, has not been so totally obliterated. But the differences between American two-party, competitive politics and those of the single party, writ so large in the American South, read only relatively smaller in other one-party areas. The overriding unity of tradition or interest underlying the single-party system often covers but lightly a number of disagreements and diversities. With no alternative party forum available, they break out in factionalism within the one party. As devices for representing and organizing social groups and interests, the faction or personal clique simply cannot contest elections, promote issues, or organize the powers of government as effectively as the conventional political party.

By contrast, the American party system offers and has offered very few examples of the multi-party system. Within some states and cities a locally strong party has vied for a time with the Republicans and Democrats. It happened in Wisconsin, for instance, in the 1930's and the early 1940's when the Progressives contested competitively with the two national parties. And within Minnesota in the same period the Farmer-Labor party, a holdover from earlier agrarian and progressive protest movements, battled on competitive terms until its merger with the Democrats. Powerful urban third parties, such as the American Labor party and the

Liberals in New York and the Socialists in Milwaukee, have also created temporary three-party systems.

The instances of American multi-party development, however, are not plentiful, and they have had little ability to survive. The traditions and expectations of a national two-party system, but-tressed by the political institutions that maintain them, undermine the local multi-party system. Both the Minnesota Farmer-Labor party and the Wisconsin Progressives capitulated eventually to the two-party system and merged with one of the two nationally competitive parties. In fact, years before there was a Wisconsin Progressive party, the senior Robert La Follette had contested within the Republican party and its primary, never wanting to venture into three-party politics. So stable and institutionalized was this intra-Republican factionalism — La Follette versus the conservative, traditional Republicans — that it replaced the more usual party competition. Democratic party fortunes in Wisconsin in the 1920's dipped so low that the party failed to carry more than 20 per cent of the legislative vote in some years. Disruptions of the usual bipolar competition of the two-party system have generally produced in the United States a bifactionalism within one or both parties rather than a drift to the standard multi-party system.

Since in the genuine multi-party system the majority party is a rarity — the German Christian Democrats between 1957 and 1961 offer one of the rare cases — the strategy of competition within them demands coalitions to capture the powers of office. The party can be content to compete for a share of power or author-ity. In the palmiest days of multi-partyism in Third and Fourth Republic France a national popular following of 5 or 10 per cent could yield even a premiership in a coalition cabinet. The Ameri-can political system with its single-member districts and its single executives — mayors, governors, and presidents — offers no divis-ible rewards for coalition-making. The American separation of legislatures and executives works against multi-partyism in a way that parliamentary systems do not.

The infrequent American multi-party systems tend to remain three-party systems. Rarely in the American experience since the Civil War do we find the fragmented, even chaotic systems of almost numberless small, doctrinaire, exclusive parties that bear such a close resemblance to the minor parties of the one- and two-party systems. The parties of those few American multi-party systems more commonly have been majority-oriented, not unlike those of the classic two-party systems. For this reason alone they tend constantly to the American two-party norm.

THE SHAPING OF THE TWO-PARTY SYSTEM

American scholars of government and political parties have not hesitated to show their preference for a two-party system. It has seemed, almost as a matter of logic, more compatible with democracy's need for majorities, responsible opposition and alternatives, and stability and structure in the political dialogue. Just as a simple matter of association, two-partyism has accompanied two of the most enduring of the democracies, Great Britain and the United States. Multi-partyism, on the other hand, has plagued some of democracy's most awesome failures, those of Weimar Germany and interwar France. The infrequent occurrence of the two-party systems has also made them seem, like precious stones, the more valuable for their rarity. This relationship between democracy and the viable two-party system has been clear enough to send political scientists scurrying in search of the causes and conditions of the two-party system. Because of the rarity of the two-party system, the search for its causes is in great part a search for an explanation of the American system.

A number of theories have been proposed to explain the special phenomenon of the two-party system. Generally they have fallen into four main categories: theories of national character, of a natural political dualism, of institutional cause, and of social consensus.

Theories of the national character have probably enjoyed the least vogue in recent years. The attacks of social science have badly damaged the prestige of national-character theories of any sort. At their worst they suggest that the excitability and volatility of the French and Latin Americans, to take a single illustration, produce a volatile and unstable party system. The moderation and deference of the British people have been said to produce a politics and party system in which reasonableness and moderation prevail.

It is implicit in these theories, of course, that the two-party systems are those of moderation and stability and that the multi-party systems are not. Taken at a less sweeping level, these explanations suggest that important social values that form a part of the country's political culture — values such as those which approve of the desirability of compromise to achieve limited ends — may affect the development of a party system. These values may, however, be merely *post hoc* descriptions derived from the observation of the political and party system; the observer, consequently, involves himself in a grand tautology. One would, I suspect, be hard put to specify some widely held political values in American life that create or even support the two-party system.

The "natural dualism" theories of the two-party systems attribute them to the natural tendency for political options to fall into alternatives: "ins" and "outs," left and right, government and opposition, status quo and change, for and against, and presumably, yes and no. A variation of the dualism theory has suggested that a prevailing sectional dualism in the United States has underlain the two-party system: seaboard versus inland frontier, then North against South, and eventually city against country. Looking at the vast number of multi-party systems and the few two-party systems, the natural dualism theory forces one to explain a number of deviations far greater than the norm. That problem aside, the theories of dualism would also suggest at least implicitly some institutional factors, such as an electoral system, which frame and give a structure to the alternatives. One may, in other words, question why the dualism should be "natural," whether it may not after all be the product of the same factors molding the two-party system or of the two-party system itself.

The institutional theorists argue, briefly, that the structure of elective offices and the election system itself are the chief determinants of the party system. In the United States, the argument goes, the focus of party politics on a single, elected President dominates the party competition. His election through the electoral college is essentially an "all-or-nothing" contest limited to national and majority-based parties. No regional or minority party can win a part of it. Furthermore, the election of legislators by plurality in single-member constituencies operates similarly, exaggerating the strength of the larger parties and denying the smaller parties any part of the victory. A party might theoretically poll 30 or 40 per cent of the popular vote over large parts of the country and still not win a single seat in the Congress.

Proponents of these institutional theories — Maurice Duverger in his *Political Parties* is unquestionably the most influential of them — also argue the converse, that proportional representation and a double system of plurality elections (the French *ballotage*) produce multi-party systems. Because these electoral arrangements reward the smaller parties with political power in the form of legislative seats, they promote a profusion of political parties. In Weimar Germany, for instance, an elaborate national pooling within the proportional representation system made it possible for a party winning only 2 per cent of the popular vote, evenly distributed across the country, to win almost 2 per cent of the seats in the Reichstag. Indeed, Weimar perfected the most equitable system of proportional representation known to the practice of government while engaging in one of the most awesomely unsuccessful experiments in constitutional democracy. That fact has not escaped the attention of the institutional theorists.

The historical evidence on behalf of the institutional theories — and they are essentially electoral-institutional theories, at that — is impressive. But contrary evidence intrudes stubbornly. The party system of the Third Republic in France remained quite unperturbed while governments experimented with a variety of electoral systems ranging from proportional representation to single-member districts. One may also wonder if some of the correlation between proportional representation and multi-party systems may not reflect the preference of those systems for electoral arrangements that would guard their interests in the status quo. In other words, might not party systems give rise to electoral systems, rather than the reverse? Finally, it is also apparent that these theories apply only to those party systems composed largely or entirely of electoral parties. They assume that a party will decline and wither if it is denied the rewards of electoral victory, an assumption that may not hold if victory at the polls is only a secondary consideration for the party.

The final category, the social theories, includes those which

maintain that the party system is shaped by the pattern of cleav-
ages and controversy in the society. When the society is deeply
riven by irreconcilable differences on fundamental social issues,
that divisiveness will be reflected in a fragmented party system. At
various times during the multi-party Fourth Republic in France,
close to 40 per cent of the popular vote went to parties that rejected the constitution itself, and a larger percentage went to
parties dedicated to basic changes in the French economy. Other
historic splits, such as the one on church-state relationships, cut
across the French electorate on other lines, none of which coin-
cided. By contrast, the societies of the two-party systems reflect
widespread agreement on such social, economic, and political fundamentals. What differences exist do so in the area of secondary
goals or over the means to achieve agreed-upon goals. The stakes
of politics are smaller, and the kinds of tolerance, compromise, and
concession necessary for a two-party system's majoritarian parties
can prevail.

Of the four contesting theories of the party system probably the
social theories best explain its fundamental determinants. All party
systems reflect directly the degree of consensus and diversity in
the society. The consensus reflected in the one-party systems con-
trasts with the social fragmentation of the multi-party society;
even the distinction between the horizontal and vertical two-party
system rests on the presence or absence of a single, overriding, divisive issue. All the party systems except the horizontal two-party
system reflect the political intensity and involvement born of great
and burning issues, crusades, and traditions. Their ideological
parties reflect and even stimulate those intense involvements. By
contrast the parties of the classic two-party systems pursue an
"easy-going," even low-pressure politics in which differences involve the less dramatic and impassioned policy alternatives rather
than fundamental institutions and ways of life. They are electoral
brokers rather than social critics.

Americans subscribe with a high degree of consensus to their
constitution, to the life of the family, to the tenets of social mobility and equality, and to a regulated, free-enterprise capitalism. The
usually troublesome relationship of church to state has partially
been eliminated from political conflict by constitutional tradition.

Political ideology and principle attract the American voters only occasionally because they have little relevance. Their political disputes, as their Presidential candidates have taken to reminding them, are over secondary goals and issues or means to generally agreed-on ends. Their political conflicts over economic and social issues have occurred in a context of consistent economic growth. Few of them have thought themselves permanently denied an opportunity for economic well-being. The economic and social fear, frustration, and pessimism behind so much of multi-partyism has not deeply influenced them. In brief, the American two-party system reflects the absence of both the unifying solidarity of the one-party societies and the persistent divisions on which multi-partyism thrives. Its politics grow out of a fluid social pluralism.

Within the broad influence of this social consensus other factors support the two-party system. Traditions and myths grow up around the two-party system and create expectations and values in its favor. A periodic change of officeholders may be desirable, the American electorate has been told, just to maintain a healthy two-party system. The institutions of the electoral system and the single executive operate with fullest force in this neutral social environment. As the major parties of the classic two-party system become more nearly pure electoral parties, they become more and more dependent on building majorities and winning elections. Their leadership and members accept the primacy of the election function; their expectations and traditions turn the party away from the styles and functions of parties in multi-party systems. Even the superficial polarities of the political conflict — the battle of ins and outs, of liberals and conservatives, of left and right — may become the traditional, and even "natural," mode of political competition. Eventually the power and expectations surrounding the well-established two-party system may be great enough to minimize and smother basic ideological differences that in other, more fluid party systems might tend to multi-partyism. The voices and goals of the far right in American politics — some of whom *do* disagree on the fundamentals of the economy, the constitution, and social equality — have been muted by the electoral majoritarianism of the two major parties.

Basically the issue is this: can political institutions such as electoral systems and patterns of elective offices filter, channel, and minimize basic social divisions so that they will be directed into two parties? It all depends, of course, on the intensity of the social differences and on the extremeness of the institutional arrangements. One could, conceivably, set higher and higher vote minima for sharing legislative seats in a proportional representation system in order to eliminate the smaller parties one by one. By so encouraging the party dualism one might, of course, run the danger of encouraging extra-constitutional political action. Generally, however, within the mandates of the democratic ethic and political stability, there are real limits to the ability of institutional structures to shape a party system.

Recent evidence about the party sub-systems within the American two-party system confirms the general relationship between the social environment and party competition. Within the American states the likelihood of two-party competition is greater in those constituencies marked by socio-economic diversity — diversity in income levels, in types of economic activity, and in social class and status, for example. Within the American agreement on fundamentals the patterns of party competition depend in part on the presence or absence of socio-economic differences on "non-fundamentals." They depend also on the pull and tug of the overall party system. The locally dormant party will be sustained by its national competitive status and the rewards it wins in other places, while the third party suffers from its failure to capture national power and influence.

NEW DIRECTIONS IN THE AMERICAN PARTY SYSTEM

Two important and related changes have recently been afoot in the American party system. For one, the minor parties and locally competitive third parties in the United States have been declining and disappearing. Second, the national pattern of Democratic-Republican competition has spread to the states and localities of the country, gradually eliminating the pockets of one-party dominance. The party sub-systems in the American federalism, in other words, more and more mirror the national two-party system. At the least this development means the loss of a rich and colorful diversity in American politics. Should their decline continue the future chapters of American party history will be the less interesting for it.

Minor parties in the American system have been of two kinds. Less apparent have been the state and local wings of a nationally competitive party, which languish as minor parties in some local sub-systems. They may not even contest elections, as the archetypical Southern Republicans did not. Many of them are perfectly content to maintain a small and closed party cadre and, thereby, a minimum of patronage claimants for the occasions on which their party captures the Presidency. Even for the vigilant minor party organization in a one-party state, presenting a full slate of candidates and providing it with adequate campaign funds, remains a perpetual problem. The party remains largely inert, excited chiefly by the power it wields in national party conventions and in the Presidential administrations its national party elects.

The second and the "classic" minor party has been the American third party: all those parties beyond the Democrats and Republicans. Within this century their strength has generally been localized, and they have at best been competitive in a single state or a small number of states. They have included the parties of broad ideology, such as the Socialist, Socialist Labor, and Socialist Workers parties, and more recently, the splinter parties of conservatism. Or they have embraced parties of a narrow set of interests — the parties of Middle Western agrarian discontent, for example — or even the single interest, such as those of prohibition and vegetarianism. At other times they have been the parties of bolters from one of the national parties. Like the Dixiecrats of 1948, who saw the advantages of preventing (by controlling Southern electoral college votes) any Presidential candidate from getting the necessary majority of electoral votes, they trade on the occasional strategic advantage or moral rectitude of an independent course.

The role the American minor party performs depends greatly on the nature of the party system within which it operates. Those in one-party systems feel the necessity to aspire to competitive status, and they often assume the duties of the chief opposition. In many ways they offer pallid and feeble likenesses of the competitive party; they remain at least largely electoral in role. But the minor party in the two-party system recognizes its electoral impotence. Since the Civil War only three minor party Presidential candidates — James B. Weaver, Teddy Roosevelt, and Robert La Follette — have polled more than 10 per cent of the national popular vote. Minor party records in state party systems are not much more imposing. They turn instead to an intense, even dogmatic, ideology and a propagandizing role. That commitment sharply restricts the party's base of support and its sources of money. They tend to a national-membership organization, with few if any levels of authority between the local, dues-paying members and a vaguely defined executive and sparse national bureaucracy. Both in function and in structure the American third party bears a closer resemblance to the interest group than to the two nationally competitive parties.

The decline of the third party in American politics has been especially noticeable since World War II. No longer do their representatives sit in Congress, and they make fewer and fewer incursions in city and state politics. The third party in the United States throughout American history has been the party of localism and regionalism. Those local pockets of strength which supported them are being slowly obliterated in the nationalization of life in the United States. The local concentrations of immigrant German Socialist strength in cities such as New York, Milwaukee, York, and Bridgeport have yielded to new generations and a new urban diversity. The quota system and other restrictions on immigration have prevented their replenishment from abroad. Similarly, the economies of the plain and prairie states no longer are dominated by the small, family farmer who formed the backbone of the agrarian protest parties. Virtually all of the third parties in American history — just as those of Canada — have had regionally concentrated strength. Their passing signals the end of those sustaining regionalisms and their atypical populations and political provincialisms.

Then, too, the states have made the electoral functions of the third parties more difficult. At least in part out of attempts to harass the Communist Party, they have made it more difficult and more costly for third parties to place candidates on the ballot. The third parties suffer also from the ever-increasing costs of campaigning in the United States, and from a growing unwillingness on the part of the mass media to extend equal time and space to their candidates and contestings. Furthermore, they suffer the same disadvantages they always have — an electoral system that puts a premium on majorities, elected executive positions that can't be divided among a number of winners, traditional and stable voter allegiances to two major parties, and a general political culture that fears that political activity on behalf of a third party is activity misspent or wasted. Above all they suffer, as do the one-party systems, from the spread of national party loyalties and competitiveness to all parts of the country and all party systems and sub-systems.

The parallel decline of one-party systems in the American states remains one of the most striking facts of postwar political life in the United States. Vermont has elected a Democratic congressman and a Democratic governor, and the Middle Western Republican strongholds have seen a Democratic resurgence. The Democratic South is no longer solid, what with Republican Presidential candidates winning more than 40 per cent of the vote in states such as South Carolina. Republican senatorial candidates have won in Texas and failed by the narrowest of margins in Alabama. In the Presidential elections of 1924 through 1936 one candidate or the other carried between 50 and 63 per cent of the states by a margin of over 20 per cent of the vote. But in the elections between 1940 and 1960 only a median of 28 per cent of the states have been captured in a Presidential election by such a margin. The two-party competitiveness so common in Presidential politics has penetrated the party systems of the states. But why?

Increasingly it is difficult to isolate and quarantine a local party system from the influences of national politics. Both the third-party and the one-party sub-system in the United States reflect a localism that is passing from American life. Radio, television, the magazines, and newspaper chains and syndicates bring the same political figures, debates, and opinions to all parts of the country, just as they bring the same comic strip or weekly drama. In the nationalization of American culture local ways of life, local identifications and pride, even local political folkways, yield their place. Increasingly, the same political symbols, the same political issues and appeals, the same political personages dominate American politics.

Even when the same set of political issues and traditions dominate politics all over the nation — as the two-party division on socio-economic status issues has since the 1930's — there have been for years states and localities in which a homogeneous population and a set of interests have embraced the coalition of only one of the parties. One-party politics have in various times and places rested on political bases of industrial labor, cotton, wheat, oil, cattle, silver, and copper. Growing economic and social diversity in all parts of the country has brought the new, diverse population base for two-partyism; urbanism in the Southwest, industry in the South, and tourism in a number of sunny states have brought some typical political changes. Formerly a single, powerful elite dominated the one-party states. Now the close challenge of new and competing elites moves them to a two-party system that can organize and express the competition of elites.

Nowhere are the shifts away from one-partyism any clearer than in the South, long the country's most illustrious region of non-competitive politics. The growing uniformity of life in the nation has invaded and softened the Southern style of life on matters of social mobility and social gentility and, perhaps, even those of race relations. The South — or the New South — has added the diversity of industry, urban working populations, and a new urban middle class. New leaders and elites challenge those of the older Southern aristocracy. For many of them, especially those who migrated from the North, the wounds and indignities of Reconstruction seem less immediate. Then, in some parts of the South the suffrage has expanded as old restrictions give way, ending in part the unreal, historic homogeneity of the Southern electorates. In these circumstances the South has increasingly felt the influences of national political currents. Southern conservatives have begun to find a home in Republicanism, and the Southern electorate responds increasingly to the issues and divisions of national social and economic politics.

The competitive counterpoint of the diverse local party subsystems, against the dominant theme of national two-party competition, has had useful consequences for that national system. In the past the ability to dominate some of the sub-systems of the states has protected a national party against annihilation. The Republican party was better able to weather the stormy years of the 1930's and 1940's because it could elect men, obtain party rewards, and hold party morale in some of the states and localities. Some observers have suggested that, consequently, the health of the national two-party system may be threatened by the elimination of "safe," one-party areas. On the other hand, it may be that party leaders whose fortunes once waxed independently of the national party will show greater concern for the cohesion and health of the national party if they must now share its failures.

A strengthening of the national parties accompanies the trend to nationally competitive two-party politics. The one-party areas have traditionally been centers of dissidence within the national parties. The state party which could isolate itself from the issues and divisions of national politics, and even isolate itself from party competition, had little need for the national party and little appreciation of its competitive problems. Its leaders, their power amplified by the rules of national conventions and by the seniority system in Congress, often fought with party leaders from the competitive sub-systems. Their decline removes an element of disunity in the national parties and strengthens, bit by bit, the central party authorities. The political forces which extend the issues and personalities of national politics to all parts of the land enhance the power of the party organizations identified with those issues and personalities.

3

The organization:
form and control

For countless Americans the political party as an organization is "the machine." Whether or not they know it at first hand, its very mention conjures up pictures of an all-powerful and ruthless boss pulling strings behind the political scenery, of a small army of ward and precinct workers leading sheeplike voters to the polls, of an inner circle of party leaders disporting themselves in smoke-filled rooms. That image of the party organization describes the turn-of-the-century urban party in the United States with the distortion, and yet the accuracy, of a caricature. It may even describe a dwindling handful of urban party organizations. But it does not and never has described the majority of American local parties.

For every virile and militant political machine in the United States there are hundreds of party organizations that cut a less dramatic figure. There are now, and there always have been, countless local county and city party organizations with inactive and ineffective local committeemen. Indeed, there are organizations with large numbers of vacancies in the committee positions.

One recent survey of four Midwestern states (Kansas, South Dakota, North Dakota, and Iowa) found one-fifth of the two parties' county committee positions vacant after the 1962 primaries, at which the committeemen were presumably elected. Even where committeemen have been formally named, the county party in reality may consist of a chairman and a handful of loyal cronies trying to fill the party ticket and to manage a desultory campaign for it. Americans who prefer a devil theory of politics will find that this picture of party organization does not conform to their deep-seated distrust of politics and the politician. It is, however, more faithful to the reality of American party organization than the image of the big-city machine.

No single stereotype even approximates the stunning diversity of party organization in the United States. Between the extremes of the machine and the "chairman and crony" organizations lie an enormous variety of other types. But for all their diversity they have in common some characteristics that set them apart from the party organizations of most of the other democratic party systems. They are semi-autonomous local organizations in a decentralized party apparatus; they are essentially skeletal organizations run by a few active partisans; and they are beset by legal controls and forms to an extent known to no other parties.

DECENTRALIZATION OF THE AMERICAN PARTIES

"Decentralization of power is by all odds the most important single characteristic of the American major party; more than anything else this trait distinguishes it from all others. Indeed, once this truth is understood, nearly everything else about American parties is greatly illuminated." So wrote E. E. Schattschneider in his classic analysis, *Party Government*. Few scholars have failed to note the same decentralization. It is and has been the touchstone of the peculiarities and vagaries of the American parties.

In no real sense do the American parties exist at the national level. Once every four years emissaries from the state and local organizations of the party do come together to select a presidential candidate in the name of the national party. The work of that convention, though, represents the state organizations performing national functions rather than any effort of a national party organization. The national committees of the major parties, nominally the peak authority in the party hierarchies, do not appoint and cannot remove the personnel of the state and local organizations. They cannot supervise or undo the tasks of the subordinate party units; the Democratic or Republican national committees would cause a great furor by suggesting that they review local party endorsements of candidates. The national parties do not control local finance. Indeed, they usually find themselves rebuffed when they propose to organize for any purpose other than service and subservience to state parties.

If authority within the American parties has settled somewhere below the peak of the hierarchy, the question is, where? At this point discussion of the decentralization of the parties often bogs down in a confusion between power and organization. We commonly assume that organization *is* power and that the terms can therefore be used interchangeably. But they are not synonymous. The major share of the power in the American party concentrates at the state levels; great state leaders and governors hold the reins at national nominating conventions and often control the party campaign funds. Party organization, however, may be virtually nonexistent — in any stable sense — at the state level. The organizational unit of the American parties is the county and/or city party. Organizationally the state and national parties are but loose conglomerations of these local parties. The fact that the local boss, the county chairman, or even the local ward captain controls virtually the only organization the party knows often enables him to resist the centralizing pressures of state or national party officials.

The reasons for this double decentralization of party power and party organization are not obscure. Since the American parties are chiefly electoral parties, party organization and function develop within the electoral constituencies. Within the American federalism, that means the states and the localities. Even though a dozen or so officials may be elected at the state-wide level, hundreds represent districts within the counties. By contrast, only the President and Vice-President are chosen in a national constituency, and in view of their selection in the Electoral College, a case can be made that no national constituency exists even for their election. Effective party organization and operation for electoral parties in a federal system demand that the parties organize locally where they can best win the largest number of those elections. The third parties do not contest elections seriously; hence they have no need for local organizations.

Other pressures work to decentralize the American parties. The incentives with which they have traditionally satisfied their workers and loyalists have been local. Especially since the triumph of merit systems in the national government service, patronage can be found only at the state and local levels. So, too, the fellowship and social status of the "court house gang" and the other social circles that have for long been a significant reward for many party minions. Finally, regulation and definition of the parties fall to the states. Their laws not only set up differing varieties of state and local organizations, but they almost uniformly create a party in which officials are selected by officials below them, down by organizational strata within the party to the popularly elected local committeemen. In such a system of indirect elections, proceeding from the ground up, few state or national leaders have popular followings or clienteles of their own.

Among the parties of the world centralization, not decentralization, is the trend. Basically the centralization of the parties in countries such as Great Britain, France, West Germany — in fact, in almost any democracy outside of the United States — reflects the centralization of governmental power. Where in a system such as the British no federalism divides and decentralizes the authority of government, where no separation of powers disperses even what central authority there is, the political system focuses political attention on the personalities, issues, and policies of national politics. The parliamentary system, with its unification of legislative and executive power, offers an additional focal point for political attention and controversy that the American system does not enjoy. The prime minister combines party leadership with governmental leadership; to centralize government is literally to centralize the party. "The Leader of any major British political party," writes Robert McKenzie, "is either a potential or an actual Prime Minister; by virtue of this fact alone, he is bound to have enormous authority over his followers whatever the checks and limitations which his party's constitution may attempt to impose on him." Furthermore, the Leader of the Opposition in England commands far greater political attention than defeated American Presidential candidates.

Governmental centralization is no stranger to the American system. The growth of power in the national government has, despite the pull and drag of federalism, begun to work some small, centralizing changes on the American parties. Presidential leadership also tends increasingly to dominate American politics and frame political issues that permeate all of American politics. The mass media not only put Presidents into living rooms all over the country; their magic is available also to legislative leaders, cabinet members, party chairmen, would-be presidential candidates, and other party notables. In this growing centralization of American governmental and political life the local issues, the local personalities, and the local styles that kept a Jim Curley or Big Bill Thompson in control of local feudalities seem less and less relevant to large numbers of citizens. The very centralizing tendencies in American life, politics, and government that are wiping out the areas of one-party and third-party rule also draw the fringes of the party closer to the center.

Furthermore, changes in the parties themselves also foreshadow a likely centralization of party authority. The sharply increasing costs of campaigning may force the parties into more highly centralized party finance. Then, too, the state and local patronage — once the provender of a decentralized party system — is fading away as the federal patronage did. As the parties become more involved with specific issues, policy and ideological incentives replace those of patronage and local favors. And today it is the national leaders and the national parties who define issues and ideologies. Local dissent and autonomy within a non-ideological party may be a nuisance and an aggravation. Within an ideological party it is heresy.

The slow trend to centralization of power within the American parties — and here we return to the distinction between decentralization of power and that of organization — need not mean the disappearance of local party organization. Even parties as highly centralized as the British build on strong, highly developed constituency organizations. Other parties have found that centralization of authority can be accomplished with a minimum of organization and central bureaucracy. The elaborate, formalized structure of the local party unit need not be duplicated at all levels in the party structure. Indeed, it may well be that with the growth of media-run and candidate-centered political campaigns that the conventional, articulated, even unwieldy party organization will be less necessary at all levels in the party.

For what power may be already lodged at the national levels of the Democratic and Republican parties, the battle for control goes on constantly. The congressional party, composed of the party's senators and representatives, has its roots deep in the local districts and precincts of American federalism. Especially since its most august and powerful figures represent the less-competitive or one-party areas of the country, it is itself the product of the localism and decentralization of the party. It stoutly resists attempts of the national committee to fashion tools — such as the abortive Democratic Advisory Council of the mid-1950's — of national leadership. The national committees, composed of delegates from the state parties and over-representing the less-populous and one-party areas, are themselves imperfect instruments of centralization. Increasingly it appears that the task falls to the President, for his is the closest to a national constituency and his is the greatest stake in national party strength. His own re-election and the success of his program in Congress depend on his ability to mobilize some semblance of national party power.

For the present only tentative and hesitant signs point to the likelihood that the American parties will bow as others have to the forces of centralization. Decentralization still marks the American major parties. In fact, it appears that the pace of centralization of governmental authority in the American federal system has far outrun any centralizing tendencies within the party system. The gap between centralizing government and decentralized parties accentuates the strained relations between a President chosen by a national party and a Congress produced by the decentralized parties.

ORGANIZATIONAL FORM: THE AMERICAN HYBRID

A good deal of the writing about political party organization since the 1950's has been influenced by Maurice Duverger's learned treatise, *Political Parties*. Many of his categories and distinctions have entered the vocabulary of political science. From a complicated and refined system of categories in Duverger's work two broad types of party organization emerge, the mass and cadre parties, each with its distinctive pattern organizational characteristics.

In the cadre, or "skeletal" parties most voters enjoy no formal affiliation with a party. The party is run by a small group of "activists," a self-selected party elite that *is* the party. The activists make its decisions, raise its funds, pick its candidates, shape its issue stands and platform, and chart its strategies. To a great extent they run an "entrepreneurial party," selling their candidates and platforms to cagey political consumers. Above all, their cadre party rests on a concept of the political party as an electoral party in which party and electorate are sharply differentiated. Since the cadre party's electoral role so preoccupies it, to the exclusion of most of the other party functions, elected officeholders often play a major leadership role in it.

The mass-membership parties, on the other hand, have tried to enroll significant numbers of voters into the party apparatus. Those members bring to the party a close identification and loyalty, a heightened awareness of the party principles, and a regular contribution to the party coffers. They bring, too, a greater skill in the dialectics of political debate, an avid and militant activity, and a general enthusiasm for party projects and crusades. The membership affiliation rarely demands much more than a signature, a few dollars a year, and an occasional expression of interest in the party. The outstanding characteristic of the mass party is, logically enough, its openness and its mystique of participation — both in the party's external encounters and in its internal processes. Unlike the cadre party its activities move beyond electing, and its organization, usually dictated by a detailed and explicit party constitution and bylaws, is more fully developed and articulated. It also generates a leadership corps of its own, which draws its power and legitimacy from the mass membership of the party.

The Duverger categories are vastly more detailed and complex than these few sentences would indicate, and yet they do not easily accommodate the American party organizations. Although they more closely approximate the cadre parties, the American local organizations have some of the features of the mass-membership parties. The urban clienteles of the city machine, tied by favors and assistance to the party, amounted almost to a membership auxiliary. They certainly did not, nor do they now, resemble the uncommitted, mobile electorate of the usual cadre party. In fact, in organizational variety the American parties run the full gamut from cadre to mass-membership party. The small-town party run by a few active officeholders and an informal elite of local notables may closely parallel the European middle-class cadre party. The new urban and suburban political clubs, on the other hand, very much resemble the mass-membership party, even to their emphasis on the "non-political" functions and their concern for intra-party democracy. Between them are all manner of permutations and combinations of each or both types. Minnesota, for example, sets up essentially cadre parties, but the party apparatus is chosen in regularly scheduled, freely advertised party caucuses open to all voters who care to come and pledge their fealty to the unspecified principles of the party. Then from these caucus attenders many ward organizations recruit a dues-paying ward-club membership.

Among the parties of the Western democracies the shift from cadre to mass-membership parties has been under way for close to 50 years. The early European Socialist and Labor parties, blessed at the outset with a unifying ideology, represented a new industrial working class that lacked every political advantage except sheer numbers. They seized on a form of organization that would at the same time assure maximum effectiveness of those numbers and meet the growing expectations for democratic participation that the older aristocratic and elitist parties ignored. They performed, additionally, large numbers of economic and social functions, all the way from sponsoring athletic and singing societies to organizing student groups and trade unions. Later, parties such as the British Conservatives, which had flourished for years as cadre parties, were forced to graft membership organs onto their traditional party structure.

The rise of the mass parties derives in part from the spread of democratic expectations in this century. Not only have electorates expanded to provide the base of support for the mass parties, but they have increasingly expected, too, that avenues of direct political participation would be open to them. The cadre party, often an aristocratic or middle-class party, had about its organization an elitist cast that grated against the egalitarian sensibilities of the new democrats. Too often the cadre party was an instrument of a self-anointed political elite that used it as a means of controlling political activity, political recruitment, and political choice. Then, too, the new mass parties reflected a change to dynamic, charismatic leadership and personalism in politics. They suited also the growing ideological involvement of the parties and the more intense loyalties that the politics of ideals and issues promotes.

The major American parties have been laggards in the development of mass-membership parties. Ideological commitment and involvement in the United States have not yet run so high that the essentially cadre parties cannot contain them. Nor have the American parties been plagued with aristocratic or upper-class domination. Little of the relationship between class elites and cadre parties seems relevant to the American experience. The American local party has been for most of its existence a party of the people. The classic urban machine embraced the aspirations and egalitarianism of the poorest city dwellers, and the organizations of men like the Byrds, Talmadges, and Longs have long had roots in the small rural farmer and worker. Indeed, the American local parties have so traditionally bound themselves to the "common people" that they have sacrificed a vast amount of middle-class respectability and good will. Moreover, the American parties have been limited in these changes, as in others, by the statutory definition of their organization imposed by the states.

In the early 20th century, when the democratic ethos was spurring the development of mass parties in Europe, the states began to impose an almost punitive democracy on the American parties. They created party organizations in neat hierarchies, constituency by constituency, from precinct to state-wide level. They often prescribed the very day and time for the meeting of state committees and conventions, often ordered specific bodies and officials to perform specific functions, and almost always outlined the process for naming the party officials. In an effort to control, even weaken, the caucus and convention system of the parties they imposed on the parties a rigid, a priori party structure, one that often had no relationship to the needs of the party and no real roots in party growth and tradition. By elevating the party's electorate into a halfway membership in the party for the purpose of choosing party officials, they blunted the demand for democratic, mass parties. They also burdened the parties with a counterfeit participation that neither solved their needs for a broader base of support nor permitted them the entrepreneurial freedom of action of the true cadre party.

These statutory parties, largely the product of a simple Progressive faith in the cures of more democracy for the ills of democracy, have lapsed into inactivity in many American communities. Often their committee positions go unfilled at the primaries for want of candidates or — even worse from the party's viewpoint — are filled by erratic handfuls of write-in votes. A number of state parties have found ways of developing mass-membership clubs and organizations outside of the formal party machinery. In Wisconsin an entirely separate, extralegal party organization has drained the statutory party of its functions and purposes. More commonly, the parties of other states have adapted the statutory organization either by adding informal leadership groups or by recruiting reservoirs of active workers. Their task in molding this statutory organization to the uses of the contemporary political party has not been easy, however. That it has been at all possible testifies to the unwillingness or inability of the electorate to exert the power and control the Progressives planned for them.

The resulting picture is one of a formal party organization in disarray and disuse. The aggressive, organizationally stable urban machine is the exception, not the rule. The fact of party decentralization has not meant that the state and local parties have been organizational paragons. The assessment of local party organization, especially of its strengths and weaknesses, depends entirely, however, on the criteria one applies. With parties as thoroughly dedicated to the electoral function as the American parties are, one is tempted to associate strength with the ability to elect candidates. That criterion, however, fails to separate the majority party that lends its name and symbols to a local notable and coasts to victory with him from the one that forges a win out of determined campaign work in both primary and general elections. Alternatively, one may look at the party organization and test its staffing, its financing, its alertness, its discipline, its cohesion. By that standard the state and local parties cut a sorry figure. Their organization is discontinuous at best, inert at worst. Discipline is slack, for the average party pleads with, rather than punishes, the recalcitrant committeeman. For lack of capable personnel and well-defined lines of authority, the organization is virtually without leadership.

For this disagreeable state of affairs the states' statutory forms need not bear the total blame. Some must be laid to a political culture that looks with suspicion on party activity, and esteems its political leadership only slightly higher than the pool-hall habitué or the numbers runner. Some of the fault, too, has to do with the decline of incentives for party action. The disappearance of patronage and preference, the tangible rewards of the job at city hall or the fixable parking ticket, have been offset only in part by purposive incentives and growing loyalties to attractive candidates.

Ultimately one must ask whether or not American politics as it is pursued and practiced in mid-century really needs explicit, highly differentiated party organizations, manned by great armies of local ward and precinct workers. That question we postpone until the end of the chapter.

THE CONTROL OF PARTY POWER

After close to a lifetime of observation and participation in the Socialist parties of Europe, a German-Italian elitist set down in 1913 a set of gloomy dicta about responsible power within the political parties he knew. We have not been able since then either to ignore or forget them. There exists within the parties, wrote Roberto Michels, an "iron law of oligarchy" which decrees that majorities are permanently incapable of running or controlling political organizations and that they must cede that power to active, expert, interested minorities.

In an argument rich with insight into mass organizations of any sort, Michels proposed that in the mass parties of the continental Socialists the demands for specialization of function, and the resulting division of labor and authority within the party, led inevitably to rule by an oligarchy of the interested and the skillful. The masses, the majority, had neither the abilities nor the taste for an active role in the affairs of the party. Organization by its very nature demanded a division into the ruling few and the many ruled. The consequences of this oligarchic rule, Michels thought, were an ideological conservatism in which the oligarchy guarded its vested interest in the ideas with which it triumphed, a tendency on its part to identify the interests of the party with its own, and ultimately, the tendency of the party oligarchs to resist replacement or to co-opt carefully prepared and equally conservative replacements.

At the same time as Michels was formulating his iron law, the American Progressives were stepping up their criticism of the boss-run, caucus-ridden parties of their time. Both Michels and the Progressives charged that the parties they knew were governed by powerful men and self-perpetuating leadership elites, often in clear disregard for the members and voters of the party. Their charges raised for their time and ours the question of the logic and wisdom of non-democratic parties as means and tools in a wider political democracy. It was the ancient dilemma of undemocratic means to democratic ends. They raised as well the possibility of achieving a significant level of intra-party democracy. The Progressives were optimistic. Michels, most assuredly, was not.

Michels wrote entirely from knowledge of mass-membership parties of proletarian ideologies. His Socialist parties really combined party and mass ideological association. As political parties they were as much, if not more, propagandizing organizations and ways of life as they were electoral combinations. Throughout the Michels book, in fact, the function of contesting and winning elections is hardly mentioned. The parties of which he speaks, concerned so intently with ideologies and a broad-gauged attack on the status quo, bear little in common with the essentially cadre parties of the United States. Michels' observations and insights for this reason apply more comfortably to large, membership interest groups such as the American Medical Association, the American Legion, and the AFL-CIO.

If one speaks of mass parties, as does Michels, the concept of intra-party democracy has the greatest relevance, for the party has a membership citizenry. But who constitutes the party and its members in the American major parties? One can, of course, develop democratic processes within the cadre, but such "intra-cadre" democracy rarely blunts the demands for party democracy. By law the American states have chosen the "party in the electorate" as a membership corps for the democratic selection of party committees and candidates. But where the voter is free, as he is especially in the American open-primary states, to decide on the spur of the moment and in the secrecy of the polling booth in which party's primary he will participate, any concept of party membership or even of party adherents collapses. The end result may be democracy or participation of a sort, but it is by persons never identified and for a party never defined.

Aside from the confusion over the participants in this party democracy, there is no consensus either about the scope or the extent of democracy within the party. Obviously, we are not unanimously willing to accept an indirect, representative democracy in which party members choose party officials and leave the governance of the party to them. Throughout the Western political parties the cry has been for direct mass control within the party of the designation of party leadership, the selection of candidates, and the writing and enforcement of the party platform, manifesto, or ideology.

Generally the issue of intra-party democracy has not agitated Americans as violently as it has the citizens of other democracies. The American attitude is most commonly that of the party "outsider" who has no deep loyalties or commitments to the party, but who would like to see its power controlled in some manner or another. He views it in the third rather than the first person. American statutory regulation of the political parties is in that spirit. It aims at control and limits, rather than internal democracy. Only where large numbers of citizens deeply involve themselves in a party, where their perspective is that of the frustrated "insider," does the pressure for internal democracy mount. Even so, it is fairly usual for partisans of one or the other American parties to accuse their opponents of bossed conventions and rubber-stamp decisions.

Within the American parties democracy, such as it is, grows from two separate systems of democratic control. There is, first of all, the democracy of the party electorate, channelled into the selection of party committees and candidates by the direct primary. That system of control has had limited effectiveness. The parties have by pre-primary recruitment and strength in the primary itself been able to nominate without enormous difficulties. Popular selection of party committeemen has more completely failed for sheer lack of interest; only rarely are the elections of precinct committeemen contested. The power of local party units and individuals over higher levels of party leadership affords the second democratic system. Its many failures and fewer successes may be appreciated by looking at the party convention, the usual instrument of that control. Within a decentralized party system such as the American, what appears in convention to be internal democracy may in reality be the struggle over centralization of party power. Local party authorities may be concerned less with the responsible control of central party power than they are with the weakening of the central party as a condition for local autonomy.

One hesitates to judge the democratic processes of the American parties, since they lack the characteristics required by a theory of intra-party democracy. They do not have the intense, participating membership group that must be placated and incorporated into the party's power system. The new membership clubs (of which, more later) do, however, make exactly these democratic demands. Second, the American parties are fundamentally decentralized. The parties of Michels' law were and are

centralized, with cumbersome central bureaucracies and powerful national leadership. Third, they are electoral parties. Michels
and the party democrats have as their main goal the maintenance
of loyalty to a party creed. Democracy, they feel, keeps the
dogma pure and powerful. And finally, the American parties are
not parliamentary parties. They have no responsibility for forming cabinets and governments as do those of the parliamentary
systems. Hence, the stakes in the control of party power are
smaller.

Yet, many of the oligarchic pressures Michels described apply
even in an electoral party. The sheer size of the American parties works against internal democracy. So does the variable level
of political interest and sophistication of their members and loyalists, even of their semi-active committeemen. So also does the
need of the purely electoral party for a tactical flexibility, a discipline, and a speed of action that only a small band of powerful
leaders can provide. And so, finally, does the expertise of leadership. Its superior experience, knowledge, planning, and interest
usually enable it to steer party conventions where and at the pace
they wish.

True intra-party democracy has rarely been achieved in any
party system. Robert McKenzie has chronicled the seeming failure of the British Labour party to fulfill its promise of democratic control. The chief reason he sees is the enormous power
of the party leader, the result of his position as prime minister or
potential prime minister. Perhaps the rarity of democracy's ful-
fillment within the parties results from an unreal standard of democracy. A naive democracy that posits the movement of consent and choice uni-directionally from the bottom to the top of
the party hierarchy no more squares with the realities of the political party than it does with the realities of democracy within
the general political system. Party members and party voters
cannot be ignored by a central party leadership, and it may be
enough that leaders must be responsive to the veto of silence, to
a possibility of a grass-roots revolt, just as they must depend on
the rank and file of the party as a source of manpower, ideas,
and influence. Those pressures we call loosely "sentiment" and
"opinion" are felt within political parties, too.

Responsibility and control within electoral parties such as the American ones grow largely out of the external control of electorates rather than from the internal control of membership. Other competing parties, by bidding for the support of a fickle voting clientele, control the unresponsive political party with the threat of electoral defeat. So also do watchful opinion media and interest groups. The reliance on external rather than internal control gives the American parties a flexibility that the democratic, mass parties cannot match. They are not encumbered by lengthy consultative processes, nor are they tied to the often inflexible views and values of bitter-end partisans. But external control through competition presupposes conditions of competitiveness that many local party systems do not offer. It also presumes a politically sophisticated electorate with some independent criteria by which to judge the alternatives and the candidates the party presents. The unresponsiveness of many urban political organizations in their heyday reflected both the absence of competition and the machine's ability, by controlling political information and socialization, to create its own unquestioning acceptance.

NEW DIRECTIONS IN AMERICAN PARTY ORGANIZATION

The reports of the death of the American urban machine may be somewhat premature, but the news of its decline over the last 30 years is not. More than any other signal its demise symbolizes the changes afoot in American party organization. As a measure of its decline the defeat of Carmine De Sapio and the Tammany tiger by the reformers in the fall of 1961 may stand as one of the great turning points in American politics.

The city machine as a type of political organization dominated the great cities of the northeastern quarter of the United States in the early decades of the 20th century. Rooted in the immigrant and first-generation populations of these industrial centers, it developed a mode of organization that for sheer discipline and mobilization of efforts may never have been equalled in the party system of any democracy. It was built around a swarm of ward and precinct workers who maintained a systematic, block-by-block contact with the voters of the area. From the local worker, the party developed upward (with a fine bureaucratic sense of "channels") to the central political leader, the "boss," of vast political cunning and virtually unlimited party power. The machine performed a broad array of services for its clientele, asking in return only its unwavering thanks at the polls. Through control of the electorate it often controlled access to candidacy and, indeed, the entire governmental apparatus, often including the courts of the city.

The fabled machine centered its life and attention on the election function. It cared little for ideologies and ideas. It specialized, in fact, in an issueless politics of immediate and tangible reward. Its only excuse for winning elections and holding power was to keep available a supply of patronage and favors with which to fill the demands of its workers and voters. The key to its success was its ability to maintain an electorate that could be "turned out" and "delivered" to the candidates and tickets of its choice. And to do that it had to deliver the goods to its insatiable followings.

The American political culture, however, no longer easily accepts either the patronage ethic that recognizes "merit" other than qualification for the job or the unthinking and unswerving loyalty (and often imperceptible abilities) of the machine's candidates. Its decline derives also from other causes. The machine created a good deal of its own supportive political culture, but now public education, the news media and opinion formers, and assorted interest groups promote other political values and perceptions. Rising levels of prosperity and relatively full employment undercut the value of the old patronage incentives. The social-service state has also pre-empted the machine's help for the poor, the sick, the unemployed, strangers to the ways of the city, the troubled, and the rejected. The fading of old ethnic and religious ties and the absorption of what were minorities into the mainstream of American life denied the machine its monopoly of avenues of social mobility and economic advancement. The old-style urban machine thrives today chiefly where there are unintegrated minorities, high unemployment, and urban poverty and misery — in areas of heavy Negro and Puerto Rican concentration, for example.

But not only the urban machine declines. Even the less

impressive and more typical party organizations of a generation
or two ago have shrunk to mere shadows of their former selves.
Atrophy has followed disuse, and rejection has followed dysfunc-
tion. James MacGregor Burns notes in a recent, widely read critique of the American parties that:

> The paramount fact about American political parties, is their or-
> ganizational weakness at all levels, from local to national. It has
> taken Americans a long time to comprehend this fact. There is a
> conventional wisdom in politics as well as economics. Generations
> of Americans have been brought up on college textbooks that con-
> trasted the weak national organization with the powerful party
> "machines" in the states and cities — even while these machines
> were disintegrating. Really strong party organizations run by
> party bosses (in contrast to the personal organizations of office-
> holders such as mayors or governors) hardly exist today.

Yet, other studies of the American electorate indicate that political activity in the United States, never at a very impressive level,
at least has been holding steady over the last generation. Seven
per cent or so of the American electorate continues to perform
some overt political activity within the year by joining a party,
contributing to campaign funds, and canvassing or electioneer-
ing. The conclusion must be that men and women continue to
participate in the political process and perform the traditional
political services. But they no longer work exclusively or largely
within the political party. Interest groups, candidate organizations and campaigns, non-partisan citizen groups, political clubs
and ideological movements, and citizen types of political groups
claim an increasing amount of their political activity.

To view the matter in another way, the political party in the
United States finds it progressively harder to monopolize its traditional political activities. The American parties have faced a
crisis in adapting to new political conditions over the recent decades, and they have not fared well in it. The traditional party
organization of the states rests on the electoral constituency; it
presupposes an electoral party in door-to-door and face-to-face
campaigning. But it is much less necessary in media- and candidate-
centered campaigns, and it is poorly adapted to the increasingly
ideological orientation of the American electorate. That function

falls more easily to the business association, the trade union, the ADA, or the conservative club. The older party organization also suffers a lack of respectability because of its earthy political style and its blunt incentive system. Neither comports well with middle-class views about the well-mannered, selfless citizen. Indeed, the paternal tone and rigid hierarchy of the usual statutory organization strike a strangely ancient note in the informal, mobile homogeneity of the suburb. Indeed, the conventional organizational forms reflect a conviction that in politics it's the party rather than the candidate that counts. But for many Americans, it *is* the candidate who counts. They will work selectively in special campaign organizations for this candidate or that, but they will not make a blanket commitment to a political party. Thousands who would balk at joining a party do not hesitate to join the Volunteers for Nixon or the Citizens for Kennedy.

But in even more direct ways the machinery of many parties is wrong for today's politics. Chosen at primaries of inflexible intervals, it resists a quick turnover in leadership, the often-necessary changing of the guard. It fails to recognize that one set of men and women may involve themselves in a presidential election, whereas quite another might become excited over a school-board campaign. It is entirely local in its orientation, representing every possible local constituency, but American political attention focuses more and more on national politics. Even the emphasis on the locality presupposes residential patterns and cohesive social neighborhoods that may no longer prevail. The individual's friendship, kinship, and occupational groups are also less and less likely to be his immediate neighbors.

For the moment, then, we see in American politics a fragmentation of political organization. Politically conscious interest groups, civic associations, candidate and officeholder followings, informal social and economic elites — and the political parties — form an unstable and ever-changing reservoir of politically informed and politically oriented individuals with a strong disposition to political activity. They move, as individuals and groups, in and out of alliance with each other for specific tasks and limited goals. Trade union joins Democratic party to elect a slate of candidates at a municipal election; civic association and community elite join Republican party leadership to support home-rule legislation; and citizens ordinarily wary of a political party join with one another to work for the election of a particularly attractive candidate. In brief, the parties find it progressively more difficult to keep within their formal organizations the recruitment and election of candidates to public office. They find it even harder to meet growing demands that they concern themselves with the statement of ideas and issues and with the management of their representatives in office.

In the face of this challenge, some party organizations have sought the springs of rejuvenation. New amateur, avocational leadership, mass-membership groups, issues conferences and study groups, and a new suburban sociability mark many of them. Parties in states such as Wisconsin and California have replaced, at least in part, some of the statutory organization with a freer, less rigid, voluntary, club-like party. In other states in which the regular parties have remained unwilling to inaugurate change, they have felt the renewed opposition of the reformers. The most notable development of this sort, the Democratic club movement of cities such as Chicago, New York, and Los Angeles, appeals to an educated, fairly prosperous business and professional group with pronounced ideological involvement in social and political issues. It has diluted the purely electoral concern of the local apparatus with heavy doses of social action, urban reformism, and conviviality. Within the party it seeks greater intra-party democracy and a renunciation of the usual patronage rewards.

What, then, for the future? The years of the 1950's and 1960's have been years of affluence and satisfaction in American politics. Any number of commentators have spoken of the disinterest, the deadlock, the immobilism of the politics of the postwar years. Political events and actors have not had great salience for most Americans; perhaps the American Negro remains the single important exception. In such a period of drift and stalemate few political issues are resolved. Certainly it is not the time for a dramatic testing of party machinery or for demands for reform and change. At the moment Americans seem willing to tolerate the mixture of the old political forms and new experiments. Campaign telethons, suburban coffee hours, and political theater parties vie with ward meetings, primary endorsements, and orotund oratory, and no one seems the worse for it.

The skill with which it performs and monopolizes the political functions remains the only test of party organization. There are no immutable criteria of organization with which to judge the political party, no changeless organizational standards that measure party efficacy. But even by a functional standard the present American party organizations fall short of success. In many American communities they share even their electing functions with other powerful individuals and political organizations. The complacent may argue that this new parity among political organizations betokens a healthy political pluralism, a greater openness of political access, a healthy competitive check on the party system itself. That may be so. But no other political organization has shown that it can offer the stable, symbolic center of political orientation, the broad and inclusive base of political recruitment, or the public responsibility (however imperfect) for its actions and decisions that the political party can. As mobilizers and representatives of democratic consent, all political organizations have not been created free and equal.

4

Issues
and ideology

THAT TIRELESS Victorian, Lord Bryce, after sur-
veying the state of the American democracy, observed that the
American parties were, like Tweedledee and Tweedledum, mirror images of each other. Other observers, less concerned with
Lewis Carroll's wonderland, have more recently voiced the same
complaint: in ideology and policy positions the major American
parties are virtually indistinguishable, and compared with other
party systems, they show a monumental disinterest in matters of
issue and ideology. In the idiom of contemporary American politics those partisans unhappy with the failure of their party to
offer a clear-cut ideological alternative accuse it of "me-tooism."

These dissatisfactions are by no means limited to the American
parties. Even among the labor and socialist parties of Europe,
long the quintessential ideological parties, one hears expressions
of a gnawing unhappiness with the parties' de-emphasis on ideology for the sake of broader electoral appeal. Intellectuals have
been meeting and writing to deplore "the end of ideology." For
it is an inescapable fact that within two- and three-party systems,

political parties find it difficult to be both ideological parties and successful electoral, brokerage parties. The electoral function demands that they integrate, compromise, and enfold large numbers of citizens into aggregates of consensus, and that they search for the least (and often vaguest) common denominator. The stating of ideologies, on the other hand, requires that the parties sharpen commitment and differences, that they set limits of value and issue to the followers they will mobilize. The incompatibility of the two functions increases, furthermore, in the party systems with a small number of competitors, for the fewer the competitors, the more inclusive the electoral party must be. This, then, is the major dimension of the dilemma: the fewer the competitive parties in the party system, the greater will be the likelihood that any one party's success in performing either of these two great party functions will be inversely related to its success in the other.

Nonetheless, one runs a risk of underestimating both the programmatic commitments of most political parties and the magnitude of the program differences among the parties of a system. The nature of the political party's commitment to goals and values differs greatly. The very vocabulary of their commitments — ideology, program, issue, interest — indicates some of the degrees and shades of difference. These varying types of commitment touch one aspect of the issue of the ideological party. A second concerns the tenacity with which the party holds to its commitments. This dimension of the controversy pivots around words such as "doctrinaire," "dogmatic," and "pragmatic." The controversy, then, is really two controversies, one over the kinds of goals the party supports and the other over the intensity of its commitment to them.

IDEOLOGY, ISSUE, AND INTEREST

The truly ideological political parties — the Marxist parties or the traditionalist Muslim or Hindu parties of Asia, for example — unite and cohere on fundamental issues of values and on an extensive philosophy and way of life. Their ideologies cover the entire range of social institutions, the fabric of basic human goals and relationships, and even the perspectives from which one views reality and human existence. They espouse a *Weltanschauung*, a full world view that exceeds what we usually think of as the merely political.

In this specific sense of "ideology," the American major parties have never been ideological. The party of extensive ideology develops in and reflects the society in which little consensus prevails on basic social values and institutions. It betokens deep social disagreements and conflicts. Indeed, the party of ideology that is also a major, competitive party accompanies a politics of almost total concern. Since its ideology defines political issues as including almost every facet of life, it brings to the political system almost every division, every difference, every conflict of any importance in society. No area of social conflict or concern escapes it. The breadth of the range of issues, the depth of its challenge to fundamental institutions, and the intensity of commitment it fosters can only lead to an impassioned, turbulent, and almost limitless politics.

Few critics of the American parties would seriously urge that they develop value and goal concerns this broad. Within the high degree of consensus and political integration in the American society, only small and perpetually non-competitive parties can build a political following on an attack on the American constitution and private capital. Yet there are differences in American society over the use and regulation of private capital, over the distribution of wealth and public costs, over basic social equality, and over the very role and responsibility of government itself. These are hardly inconsequential matters, and many of them touch what most people would call the social and political fundamentals. As the raw material of the partisan politics of many democracies, they are generally debated in terms of policy proposals. A party advocates social security or price control rather than the redistribution of wealth, a law forbidding discrimination in employment rather than justice or equality. It is at this level of issue and program that the critics of the American parties charge that they fail.

The Democratic and Republican parties do take issue stands. They advocate different programs of price supports for farm commodities, federal aid to education, medical care for people over 65, and regulation of labor-management relations. Their partisans and identifiers also hold differing views on policy questions. What, then, is the complaint? In what ways do the American parties fall short of being programmatic? The indictment is a long and varied one. Their critics would like to see them take more sharply differing stands on the same issue, and they urge them to adopt positions on a greater number of issues — on all the major issues that agitate significant numbers of Americans. They urge them to speak out unambiguously on all these issues, to take the lead in shaping attitudes on basic social problems, to campaign on them and organize support behind policy alternatives. They would, furthermore, like the parties to choose leaders and candidates loyal to the party's program. Finally, the more sophisticated urge a greater consistency in their treatment of issues; they would argue that the American party's tendency to offer something for everyone produces a grab bag of positions on issues whose basic assumptions or goals often conflict. They seek political parties that will adopt policies dictated and unified by a stable set of underlying values — those syndromes of goals or attitudes they may call liberalism or conservatism.

Issue proposals that are too moderate and too few, that are too timidly proclaimed and too laxly enforced, too changeable and too inconsistent — these are the charges. The American parties mute rather than declaim the issue differences in the American political system. They put forward issues and programs, not out of an a priori commitment to them but because they are good bait for the electoral nets. Yet the American parties are not without issue commitments — indeed, no party is. The American parties, in fact, suggest the minimum ideological component (and the reasons for it) which one finds in even the most pragmatic electoral party.

Each of the American parties has its implicit political and social ideology. Each accepts the political system, the prevailing social and status systems, the economic system, and economic institutions. The program disagreements between them on farm price-support legislation, for example, reflect a vast ideological agreement on basic matters ranging from a free-enterprise economy to belief in the social value of the family farm. Even when a party's acceptance of a basic ideology is tacit and implicit, it acts as a powerful educational instrument on its behalf. Party oratory, party platforms, and party appeals are couched in the verbiage and symbols of the ideology; party leadership identifies with it. Where, as in the American party system, the parties subscribe to almost the same fundamental ideology, they reinforce the social consensus and sustain the existing limits to political debates.

Divisions between the American parties occur at a more specific policy level — at the level of dealing with unresolved ideological issues, or more likely, in disagreements over means to agreed-upon ends or on the meaning of vaguely defined ends. Democrats and Republicans divide on policies toward labor and agriculture, on governmental efficacy in managing and regulating the economy, on the use of monetary and fiscal policies, on the nature of the nation's international commitments, and on the general role and scope of government. Behind these policy differences is each party's "silent ideology," the constellation of policy interests of the party's stable, continuing electorate. The fact that the Democratic party has built a national coalition of urban, lower socio-economic and minority groups lies beneath its espousal of a wider social-welfare program than the Republicans have favored. Even the large brokerage party, in seeking electoral aggregates by minimizing differences, builds its coalitions around a nucleus that distinguishes its electorate from that of its competitor.

The commitment of the major American parties to a constellation of interests may, in fact, be stronger than we give it credit for. Many of the voter loyalties within the American electorate that appear to be traditional, old-line party loyalties, are in reality loyalties to this silent, implicit ideology of interest. The man who votes for the Republican party because his family always has, or because his friends do, may be voting for a distant, traditional, unspoken ideology or interest that has been transmitted to him as he first learns about the political world. Voting for the party of one's father may be, considering the stability of social and economic status between generations, ideological voting one generation removed. The vague support a traditional voter gives to the Democratic party as the party of the "little man" or the "common man" acknowledges in a verbal short cut that same ideology of interest. It is in this sense that James Burns refers to the American major party as "instant ideology." It sums up, personalizes, and transmits a stable pattern of political interests.

In the democracies of the mature industrial nations the parties tend overwhelmingly to divide electorates on socio-economic status lines. The parties espouse social and economic policies that reflect the interests of their clienteles. Control and sharing of the gains, rewards, and costs of industrialism become the overriding political issues. Within the American parties this alignment of the parties on socio-economic lines sharpened in the late 1920's and the 1930's. Its final triumph marks the greatest partisan impact of the Rooseveltian revolution. The Democratic coalition of the South and the urban proletariat, racial and ethnic minorities, and the generally underprivileged has dominated American politics since then, although with some weakening in the '50's and '60's. The Republicans have built largely on the electorates of rural, Protestant, Anglo-Saxon, and middle- and upper-class America.

The two American party coalitions — and the silent ideologies they exude — have hardly been cohesive, nor have their lines been clear or orderly. The magnitude of differences on issues between them has not been great. At one point, indeed, it appeared that the future of two small volcanic islands off the coast of China would dominate the issues of the 1960 Presidential campaign. The American parties spell out policy stands tentatively and vaguely. They do not have a flair for enunciating principles, nor do they speak in one clear ideological voice. They do, as their critics charge, bow before all the limits the political system sets to their statement of programs and ideologies. But of the charge of disregarding interest and policy issues altogether they are not guilty.

THE LIMITS OF IDEOLOGY

The necessity of winning elections stands as the greatest barrier to ideology in the political party. Depending on the nature of the system in which it competes, the party must appeal to the 5, 10, 25, 35, or 50 per cent of the electorate it must gain to remain competitive. If it is content to remain a minor party or a party of limited electoral success in a multi-party system, the conflict between the electoral and ideological functions is minimized. But for major parties like the American ones, committed to a contest for national majorities, the dilemma exists in its most harassing form.

But to speak of the electing function as a limit to the statement of ideologies and issues is only to beg the question. Under what conditions does the electing function conflict most seriously with the ideological? The conflict increases as the percentage of the electorate the party must appeal to increases, and the more heterogeneous the society in which it functions the greater the conflict. Since they must build majority coalitions in a very heterogeneous society, the American parties, were they to become truly ideological, would have to find some axis, some line of separation, on which to divide the American electorate. In a two-party system the politics of ideology must be uni-dimensional. The parties must find the single issue or the single pattern of issues and goals that great numbers of citizens will recognize as the one of surpassing importance and the one on which they are willing to be separated into two great camps. Ideological parties must be able to take unequivocal stands on a number of issues (Table 3-1). To do so, their stands must rest on an electorate composed of individuals whose interests or whose over-all guiding ideology leads them to those same stands or to disinterest on some and support on others (Table 3-2).

In the American plural society, however, individuals in the electorate do not divide into two great patterns of interests or ideologies. Large numbers may join in support of alternative A_2 in issue A, but they may divide on issue B, some behind B_1 and some in favor of B_2 (Table 3-3). Overlapping group memberships, experience, and loyalties cut through and across the American electorate. Two union officials may favor A_1 if issue A concerns labor legislation, but as Catholic and Jew they may disagree if issue B concerns aid to parochial schools. Furthermore, American voters have no single priority system, no single scale of utility in politics. For some voters issues of collective bargaining or aid to education predominate; for others it may be defense policy or disarmament. The parties cannot, therefore, establish any orderly priority of commitments.

If that confusion of cross-cutting issues and value preferences were not enough to confound the two national parties, the geographical distribution of the American electorate would. Where electoral differences are not spread evenly over the extent of the political system and where the electorate of one region differs in composition and outlook from that of another, the political debate differs from region to region. Where those two variations are codified and institutionalized by a federal system, the limit to ideology is all the greater. Various state parties of both the national Democratic and Republican parties differ in ideological composition and in priority rating of issues. These variations within the federal system produce the anomalies of a Harry Byrd to Wayne Morse span within the Senatorial Democrats and a Barry Goldwater to Jacob Javits span within the Republicans.

SCHEMA OF THE IDEOLOGICAL AND NON-IDEOLOGICAL PARTIES

Table 3-1 IDEOLOGICAL

Issue	Party X	Party Y
A	A_1	A_2
B	B_1	B_2
C	C_1	C_2
D	D_1	D_2

Table 3-2 IDEOLOGICAL

Voter	Party X	Party Y
1	A_1 B_1 C_1 D_1	A_2 B_2 C_2 D_2
2		
3	A_1 D_1	
4		C_2

Table 3-3 NON-IDEOLOGICAL

Voter	Party X	Party Y
5	B_1 D_1	A_2 C_2
6	A_1 C_1	B_2 D_2
7	B_1	C_2
8	D_1	B_2 C_2

In an electorate that divides in an almost infinite number of issue permutations and entertains an equally large number of potentially conflicting interests, the competitive party must rely on non-ideological appeals — the attractive candidate, for instance — or on pseudo-ideological symbols, platitudes, or truisms to hold its disparate electorate together. The American parties become great neutral electoral brokers, whose art and skill is in the minimization of difference and division. They profess few deep or lasting issue commitments of their own; they tend instead to judge an issue by its pragmatic value in organizing voter support. Their role in a competitive two-party system demands an emphasis on consensus and agreement, on the widely held political pieties rather than on the issues that divide men.

So far we have proceeded as if every American voter had a concern, even sporadic and half-hearted, for political issues and ideologies. They do not. For a large chunk of the American electorate issues and ideologies have little salience, and their disinterest in ideologies limits sharply the extent to which the party can afford to speak in ideological appeals. The voters, even the members, of a political party have far less ideological involvement than do the leaders, whose ideological concern is one of the main reasons why they have been attracted to party activity. The ideologists, in other words, are already the party activists and the strong party identifiers. Issues and ideology require verbal facility, background and knowledge, attention and interest, and a political sophistication that are not common among the population as a whole. The capsule slogan and flashing smile capture far more political attention in the electorate than the windy manifesto or the sober discussion of political philosophy. Indeed, studies of the American voter suggest that a significant number make their choice of party or candidate in a campaign and then rationalize their candidate's stands to comport with theirs. If he favors federal aid to education and they do not, they will perceive him as opposing it.

So, it is hard to find in this complex American electorate the stuff of ideological, two-party politics. Some voters do see the socio-economic issues and loyalties as the most significant. They would heighten and accentuate the politics of class conflict. But many others do not see the American society in those terms. Traditional American mores support their belief that there are no significant class lines and that there are no significant limits to equality and opportunity. What conflict there is in American society — and a politics of ideology *does* imply conflict — they may see as results of politicians' "stirring up" an otherwise content and harmonious populace. Voters who reject socio-economic politics may be impelled by other ideologies: humanism or Christianity, egalitarianism, a belief in the imperatives of world peace and order. Others may be brought to the party by old family ties, the urging of a spouse or local ward captain, the promise of a political job or reward, lingering sectional or community conformities, or the appeal of a Presidential candidate. Indeed, no party appeal undercuts the ideological orientation of a party quite as surely as the personal appeal of a popular candidate. Patronage and personalism have combined in the traditional style of American politics — whether in the Northern cities or the Southern states — to drain the electorate and, thus, the parties of even the most modest ideological orientation.

The limits to ideology are not altogether a matter of the social composition and political socialization of the American electorate, however. The American federal system as a limit has already been mentioned. Interest groups in the United States are not anxious to see the parties become more ideological, for it would mean that the parties would commit interest groups, more or less as satellites, to one or the other party. The powerful interest groups in the American political system would prefer, generally, to keep access open to each political party. For this reason organized labor has little taste for any talk of an American Labor party, and it may, in fact, rue its strong commitment to the Democratic party. For strategic reasons the interest group, in other words, would rather use the parties for limited objectives than become some party's permanent accessory.

THE IDEOLOGICAL TRICHOTOMY

The political party presents not one ideological image, but three: the ideology of the party militants and workers and leaders, the public ideology of the party's platform and candidate appeals, and the ideology of the party's voters. Ideological crises or inconsistencies within a political party generally involve some difference within or among these three ideological spokesmen about the importance of issues or the nature of the party's stand on them.

Party factionalism has long sprung from ideological divisions among the party militants and leaders. The history of Marxism and socialism throughout the world is largely such a history of schism and heresy; the various American socialist parties are but distant repercussions of that warring. These factional disputes have been with the American major parties, too, though in less exacerbated form. Liberal and conservative wings contend within both of them, often breaking into bitter enmity at national nominating conventions. In fact, the initial factionalism in American politics, out of which the Federalists and the Jeffersonians formed, grew out of differences about the new nation's role in the world, the basic form of the emerging political institutions, and the role of government in the growth of the national economy.

This sort of intra-party ideological factionalism points to an aspect of ideology that we frequently overlook — that it performs valuable functions within the party organization as well as in the electorate at large. With the decline of patronage and material rewards, ideology and issues increase in importance as incentives for work in the party. That means, in effect, that the party actives and workers are far better attuned than the party voters to the ideological reference and argument, that their satisfactions depend more on the triumph of idea and issue. It is ideology, oftentimes, that keeps them active in the party rather than in the Elks, the PTA, or the United Fund campaign. Candidate and platform appeals to ideology may often be intended, as a result, more for the party workers and contributors than for general consumption by the electorate. The American parties may be forced, if they want to maintain the organization an electoral party needs, to concern themselves with issues often enough to achieve maximum organizational cohesion and morale, but not so often as to impair the breadth (and innocuousness) of its appeal to the external electorate.

The split ideological image may, alternatively, result from differences between the positions of the party leadership and actives on the one hand and the party's candidates and platforms on the other. To some extent this has been the trauma of the Republican party since the 1930's — the distance between the private and the public ideologies of the party. By now it is no secret that the majority of officials and actives within the Republican party have been privately ill at ease with the liberal, moderate, progressive, or "new" Republicanism of their platforms and candidates since the 1930's. Their hearts remain well to the right of their candidates, and they would have preferred Presidential candidates such as Taft and Goldwater rather than Willkie, Dewey, Eisenhower, and Nixon. Every four years they have accepted grudgingly the necessity for such a compromise with electoral necessities, hoping they would not be asked to do it again.

Beneath such a split between the party's private and public ideologies lies a common division between the party leadership and the party's public office-seekers. The party worker has often been recruited into party service by ideological inducements, but candidates and officeholders consider the party an electoral organization rather than an ideological vehicle. They are impatient with any concern of the party's that might compromise its electoral mission. So, to return to the illustration of the national Republicans, at the national nominating conventions the pressure for liberal candidates and platforms builds up among the Republican governors, congressmen, and local officials as they calculate the impact of the party national ticket on Republican electoral chances everywhere. Within most of the parties of the democracies, in fact, this ideological gulf prevails between party cadre and party candidates. The ideologically oriented occupy the political left and right, and the less ideological candidates whose implicit ideology is a commitment to the status quo pre-empt the center. Within the British Labour party the political radicalism of the members of the constituency organizations has long been the despair of the party leadership and parliamentary party — hence Beatrice Webb's exasperated observation that the constituency delegates at national conferences were "fanatics, cranks, and extremists."

Confusion and chaos also develop when the ideological tone of the party's leaders and their public appeal differs from that of the electorate that supports it. That problem has burdened the liberal Catholic parties of Europe since World War II. They built a political ideology on the social-justice encyclicals of Popes Leo XIII and Pius X as an answer other than socialism to middle- and working-class demands for social reform. Their electorates — often seeing them only as opponents of communism or as the party of the Church's historic ties to the status quo — have been much more conservative. To some extent the American Democratic party has faced the same problem. Large numbers of its voters, attracted by Southern regional ties, old Irish and Italian Catholic loyalties, or by the temptations of patronage, have not supported its professed positions on social-welfare legislation and civil rights. The party, much as the Catholic parties of Europe, finds it more than usually difficult to enact its programs.

That ideological dilemma emerges from the failure of the party's electorate to perceive the party in the ideological terms the party proposes. The recent work of Herbert McCloskey on the ideologies of the American parties and their voters suggests that the militants and leadership of the two parties differ more sharply and in general show a greater ideological awareness than do their party electorates. Such evidence hardly supports the critics of the parties, who argue that there are ideological currents within the American electorate that the major parties and their candidates suppress. Rather it would appear that the parties, often at the insistence of their leaders and workers, take stands and positions that are meaningless or inconsequential for large numbers of Americans.

The problem of developing a political ideology rests, for the American parties as for all others, on one basic organizational fact and two additional facts about ideology:

1. For ideological purposes, the political party is really three parties: the organizational cadre, the candidates, and the electorate.
2. Within any one of these components or between any two of them:
   a. there may be ideologically oriented individuals and non-ideologically oriented individuals, or
   b. there may be individuals oriented to ideology X, those oriented to ideology Y, ad infinitum.

The possibilities for difference and disagreement, especially for the majority party operating in a vast and complex plural society, are almost limitless.

INSTRUMENTS OF IDEOLOGY

Party organization develops basically in response to the roles and functions the party performs. The parties of ideology throughout the Western democracies specialize in the periodic party meeting, the party headquarters and reading room, study clubs and research organizations, party newspapers — these and other organizational forms and techniques beyond those needed by the purely electoral party. That the American parties lack them both reflects their past electoral concerns and indicates their present organizational unreadiness for an expanding ideological role.

Beyond adapting its formal organization for the purposes of advocacy and teaching, the classic ideological party has welcomed the ideologue and intellectual to party activity and leadership. Ideology is verbal, couched often in cloudy and forbidding rhetoric, and it is abstract and philosophical. From the days of Burke and then Marx down to the present, the leadership of the European ideological parties has been graced by a steady stream of notable academics and literateurs, men such as George Bernard Shaw, Harold Laski, Léon Blum, and Jean-Paul Sartre. Within the American parties even a thoughtful and literate Presidential candidate such as Adlai Stevenson has been viewed, with mixed distrust and amusement, as an "egghead."

The American parties specialize in the episodic, minimal activity of the electoral party, and they lack the organizational traditions of the ideological party. Ideological parties sponsor a series of auxiliary groups, such as youth groups and labor unions, not only to secure party members and voters, but also to educate their people into the party creed and to mobilize their demands for party purposes. The few auxiliaries of the American parties — the women's organizations, the minorities divisions of the national committees, and the Young Democrats and Young Republicans — appear to be much less the instruments of the parties' educational purposes. They often appear, in fact, to be organizational devices for softening the parties' unwillingness to admit these groups to full leadership and participant status. The American parties certainly do not employ them as means for representing or co-opting the interests and ideologies of sub-groups, for they are really campaign rather than educational devices.

The full organizational panoply of the ideological party reflects its attempt to control or monopolize the instruments of ideology within the political system. But the American parties have never dominated, much less monopolized, ideological expression in the American system. Interest groups traditionally speak for issues and interests in the American legislatures and administrative process in the absence of party stands and party discipline over its elected and appointed representatives. They are of many varieties. Large groups such as the AFL-CIO and the American Bar Association pursue many of their goals without resort to political activity, but on occasion they may be forced to speak politically for their interests. As the scope of government action expands sharply, as it has in the past generation, voluntary associations such as these are brought more and more directly into the range of politics as spokesmen for powerful interests and ideologies. The *ad hoc* political interest groups, created solely to engage in political activity on behalf of a single interest or policy, are often front groups for better-known interest groups that see the wisdom in anonymity. Finally we have always had non-party groups representing a systematic, full-blown political ideology; today they are typified by the Americans for Democratic Action and the vast galaxy of conservative clubs, parties, alliances, and movements. Their very existence acknowledges the inability of the American party system to absorb all the ideological currents abroad in the American polity, for in many multi-party systems these ideological groups would be separate political parties.

The relationship between these groups and the American major parties can be taken as some index of the parties' ideological involvement. So long as the relationship is distant, suspicious, standoffish, the parties cannot take a role of ideological leadership. But recently a number of American interest groups have involved themselves more closely with the parties. Organized labor, once committed to Eugene Debs' policy of independence of the parties so that labor could freely reward its friends and chastize its enemies, has tied itself to the Democratic party. Employer and business groups have allied themselves with the Republicans. Among the farm organizations the National Farmers Union almost un-failingly supports the Democratic party, and the American Farm Bureau Federation the Republican. To the extent that a party receives and accepts the support of a number of interest groups — accepts their public endorsement, money, and campaign help — it commits itself to the groups' interests and ideologies. And as these commitments grow, the party becomes less and less the traditional brokerage party, less and less the bargainer and auctioneer among political interests, and more and more the representative of a set of interests.

Political parties do not become full-blown programmatic parties by pushing aside their electoral traditions and "getting religion." The ideological party operates with the support of special organizational instruments and traditions. And if a political party is to be genuinely committed to ideology or program, committed to it for more than its usefulness as an electoral appeal, it must participate in the processes of political education and socialization. It must have the traditions, the spokesmen, and the devices by which it can reach large numbers of citizens with its program. It must to some extent mold its own electorate. It must as well cultivate among its voters the heightened awareness of politics, the political knowledge, the degree of involvement, and the reinforcing frame of reference so crucial as a base to personal ideology. By these criteria, one must confess, the American major parties afford very imperfect vehicles for the development of a fuller ideological component.

THE AMERICAN PARTIES: TOWARD IDEOLOGY?

Shortly after his defeat in the 1948 Presidential election, Thomas E. Dewey argued that an ideological intensification and realignment in the American party system was unlikely to happen because, among other reasons, not enough Americans would confess permanently to conservatism. The party choosing to be the conservative party would, therefore, be doomed as a permanent minority. Conservatism is, however, less of an anathema in the 1960's, and its resurgence makes the Dewey argument less compelling. Its new favor has also raised again the possibility of aligning the present two American parties into more homogeneous ideological camps — one to be, inevitably, liberal and the other conservative.

The possibility of greater ideological involvement for the Democratic and Republican parties does not concern only the place of program in American politics. It also holds the key to other changes and developments in the American party system. The development of centralized parties and mass-membership party organizations in the United States depends on the degree of involvement with issues the American parties can generate and sustain. Ideology alone will provide the impetus and incentive for those changes in the form and organization of the parties. Those structural changes in the long run follow changes in political motive, incentive, and task — the goals and expectations the party actives and electorate express.

Realignment in the American party system on socio-economic class lines began in the Presidential elections of 1928 and 1932. State party lines have slowly but inexorably moved into rough alignment with the national parties. The parties of some states held out for decades, Pennsylvania until the 1950's, the Southern states until the 1960's. Further realignment must proceed along two fronts. First of all, the parties must find a basis for division, either by developing the socio-economic differences along differences in income and social status, or by finding a new one. The first possibility seems the more likely, with the resurgence of frank liberal and conservative identification built essentially on social and economic policy differences, and with the triumph of national coalition lines in the once-solid South. That line of division will also be strengthened if the present unequal sharing in American "affluence" continues, if luxury housing and swimming pools grow along with the unemployment rate. There is always the possibility, however, that some dramatic national event or crisis, equal perhaps in political potency to the stock-market crash and the great depression, might provide the new overriding dimension of political debate and difference. It is not inconceivable that after a stunning national defeat or loss of an international objective — the loss of a limited war, the loss of the race to the moon, a dramatic loss of weapons superiority or parity — that the parties might re-coalesce on foreign policy or defense alternatives. But for the moment the division of socio-economic politics appears to offer the best focus for alignment.

It is not enough, though, to increase popular awareness of and attention to the focal dividing issue. The development of ideological parties depends on maintenance of the supremacy of that issue and the subordination of other ideological forces in American politics. Since World War II a subsidiary ideological axis, one on international commitments, has repeatedly cut across the socioeconomic status lines dividing the parties. Groups in both parties have been committed to American foreign aid and to American obligations throughout the world, and each party has also had its heirs of the earlier isolationists who favor fewer American ties and activities in the world. President Eisenhower, discouraged by the resulting fragmentation of party lines, once thought of the possibility of founding a new political party which would accept a role of leadership in world affairs for the United States, but which would be committed to a conservative role for government in the economy.

The advocates of ideological alignment, of both the political right and the left in the United States, clearly underestimate the difficulty of reaching this goal. The partisans of the left and right commonly trade on two assumptions, both of which are questionable. They argue that there is in the American electorate a great aggregate of ideologists who need only the stimulus of an unabashedly liberal or conservative party appeal to emerge. Therefore, no conflict exists at all between the electoral function and the programmatic function. All evidence, however, indicates that the political awareness and involvement of the American electorate in ideologies falls somewhat below these expectations. The ideologues of the right also assume that the Democratic coalition of minorities, urban workers, and lower socio-economic status groups is breaking up and that, consequently, the chances look bright for a national conservative majority. Indeed, the changes within the South, the flight to the suburbs, and the absorption of the old minorities into the mainstreams of American life do threaten the old Roosevelt coalition. But there is no reason to assume that two-party competition in the American system centers on a fixed line of battle, a permanent pair of coalitions. No party threatened by the declining effectiveness of its old appeals will continue to fiddle the old airs and tunes while Washington burns. The comparable folly of the liberals has been to feel that little has changed and that the old appeals have lost none of their magic effectiveness.

Even though there is little clamor for the American parties to develop wide-ranging ideologies or total programs of action, they will probably increase their attention to program and issue. The result will surely be a disrupted, discontinuous, and often contradictory programmatic emphasis. It seems unlikely, however, that the slow trends of the last generation will be halted; program has come to stay in the parties. Working against all the still-powerful limits to ideology in the parties is the growing importance of ideology in the internal organization and operation of the party, the increasing political awareness and education of the American electorate, and the growing degree of ideological awareness promoted by interest groups and other non-party political communicators. Basically, though, the raw materials of ideological or issue-oriented politics are the needs and demands of a mature and complex society for which large numbers of citizens seek government action and solution. The very concept of ideological politics makes no sense when it is applied to limited, negative government. With the growth of the governmental role and power in the United States, the materials exist for governmental action and for party policy attitudes and programs. Within the American political system those raw materials have been present for the very short time — short as the time of political movements and currents is measured — of one generation.

Will the increasing ideological component of American politics, though, be for the good? Whole schools of thought have argued that question, for we have had a sharp division, too, on what one might call the ideology of ideology. Ideological parties are by their nature parties of change and of alternatives to the status quo. The cries for more ideological parties have come from people in American life dissatisfied with that status quo and with the support the non-ideological parties tacitly give it. The defenders of the parties and their preoccupation with the electoral function tend equally to be content with the parties' minimization of social conflict and with their support of the status quo. Behind their rationale and praise for the brokerage party rests an unstated major premise: the avoidance of social conflict is the highest goal a political party can achieve. The brokerage party, through its compromising and accommodating operations, achieves it; the ideological party does not.

As challengers of the status quo, the ideological parties reflect social conflict and social differences. At the least their proponents believe the expression of conflict will lead to its resolution more effectively than to its suppression. All this seems clear. When one finds parties and a party system that are distinctly non-ideological, it is easy, too easy, to assume that they are what they are simply because they reflect a basic social consensus that leaves no room for ideological politics. Since there are no ideological parties and no ideological politics, there must be no deeper social conflicts or divisions. Such a simple, one-to-one, one-way relationship is tempting. One easily yields to the conclusion that the American parties have eschewed ideology because of the prevailing social consensus in the American society. That supposition does have plausibility to recommend it. Parties do reflect divisions in society rather than create them. They do not, as middle-class Americans often figure, go about pitting Americans against Americans to create political conflict on which they may, like vultures, feed and sustain themselves. But such a position pays insufficient deference to the ability of the political party to suppress or accentuate political conflict.

The traditionally ideological party may through its educational power and its control of the political symbols and involvements be able to intensify political differences. It may seize on lingering rivalries and frustrations to intensify political involvement and emotion, or it may broaden the areas of political conflict and introduce elements of intransigence and even fanaticism into the political system. As the facts of this century indicate, the political party is quite capable of becoming a great, impersonal, even institutionalized demagogue. On the contrary, the American parties skillfully suppress that conflict. By means of their duopoly of the American political market, they can close the conventional avenues of political debate to ideology, forcing it to unorthodox platforms and occasions. By associating themselves with the status quo they transfer its legitimacy and acceptance to themselves. Their power to determine what will be talked about and what will be argued, what is possible and what is not possible, involves the power to define what is extreme and who the extremists are. The extremists often turn out, almost by definition, to be the ideologists — those men of uncompromising commitment to principle and goal.

That quietism which sees the non-ideological party as the symbol of a "happy society" often leads to another slippery proposition: if the party can function more effectively without reflecting or carrying a burden of program or ideology, so too can the political system. It may be, given the vast range of impediments to their becoming more programmatic, that the American parties cannot operate in a manner very different from their present one. But one cannot from that conclusion make the quick leap in deduction to argue that, concerning the well-being of the political system and the society, such an outcome is a good one. What is good and functional for the parties may not be good for the political system as a whole; any such assumption comes close to placing the political party as a prime value in the political system. The question of the capacity of the political system for managing conflict, and of its responsibility for managing it, is entirely another matter.

If the parties in the United States do not frame issues or promote a debate in programs and values, who is to do so? Or has the American political system no need for clarification of basic values and no need to resolve basic social differences? Certainly there is no call for parties which would espouse vast ideologies of the scale of the socialists or which would conduct continuous seminars in political philosophy. There are, however, groups and individuals in the United States who argue that their own deeply felt programs and values find no hearing in the two parties, that in effect the parties throttle debate not only in social, economic, and political fundamentals, but in a good many of the areas of public policy, too. It is possible to argue that the interest groups will provide an outlet for them — just as they provide an organizational alternative to the parties — but they suffer the basic infirmities of privacy, instability, and exclusiveness. As publicly responsible organizations in a democracy they bring far fewer advantages to the political arena than do the parties.

Perhaps the programmatic problem of the democratic political party can best be summed up as a function of that democracy. The major American party is faced with the constant necessity of balancing its electing and its programmatic roles. Does it make its most effective contribution to democracy by aggregating majorities, by compromising differences behind candidates, by suppressing disruptive conflict? Or does it better serve democracy by educating the electorate, by framing issue alternatives for it, by illuminating choice, and by affording a means to common goals? At the philosophical level most of the debate over ideological and non-ideological parties centers on that issue.

5

The structure
of incentives

THE POLITICAL party has another, less obvious aspect behind the façade of its external image and its political functions. Internally it is a vast network of personal ties, authority relationships, and incentives to activity. Basic to these relationships are the rewards and sanctions, the political incentive system, which the political party commands and manages. If the party is to continue functioning as an organization it must make "payments" in an acceptable "political currency" adequate to motivate and allocate the labors of its workers.

To continue the analogy to economic organization, each party worker or participant will continue his participation in the party organization only as long as the utility of the incentives to him exceeds the cost to him of the labors the party expects in return. But, although we know a great deal about the effectiveness of economic incentives in allocating labor and resources, the nature and role of the incentives for political activity are less obvious. What inducements recruit men to activity within the political party? Why do they recruit some men and not others? What goals is the party activist trying to satisfy? To these incentives that bring men into the party and hold them together in a complex, highly differentiated organization we turn in this chapter.

THE INCENTIVES

The incentives that recruit activity for the parties are far easier to describe in the aggregate than they are for individual partisans. They are not fixed and immutable. The attractiveness of a patronage job may wane, and it will certainly differ from individual to individual. Nor does any party organization build entirely on any one incentive. The set of incentives that attracts national party leadership may have no power to attract the efficient ward chairman, and the reverse is equally likely.

The incentives that produce party activity in the United States do not differ greatly from those in any other party system. But since this is more particularly a discussion of the American parties, it may be appropriate to begin a list of incentives with the one most specifically associated with them: the incentive of *patronage*. The word means the appointive positions in government awarded either for past political services or in expectation of future work. The patronage positions available to the American parties range from janitorial jobs in city hall to ambassadorial posts, and from a local street inspectorship to a seat on the Federal bench. Sometimes the concept of patronage is extended to cover the honorary titles, honors, and non-remunerative positions government can bestow. These positions, of which the Kentucky Colonel may be the American archetype, carry only the coin of prestige and status. No party system has so systematically depended on patronage as the American. Even today, though merit systems cover most of the Federal administrative establishment, a number of state and local bureaucracies remain for the rewarding of the party faithful.

At other times the concept of patronage has been used to encompass immediate, tangible rewards other than those of government employment. These rewards, which one may call *preferments*, are those which can be granted administratively, and thus expeditiously, by a party that controls the executive or administrative patronage-holders. They are grants of extraordinary treatment by government. The active partisan or financial "angel" may seek contracts for printing the plethora of forms and stationery that government agencies devour annually, or contracts for the construction of public buildings, roads, or parks. Local governments, especially, spend vast sums every year in capital improvements; that fact probably best explains the unusual interest of the American construction industry in local politics in many parts of the United States. Preferment may also take the form of special treatment in public services — the repaved stretch of road near the farm or home of the party functionary, for example — or in administrative decisions, such as those admitting patients to public hospitals and institutions.

The incentive of the *political career* may also attract men to party service. Especially where the party can control the nominating process, it may permit only party actives to be candidates for public office. Any ambitious would-be candidate must find access to the party ticket through activity within the party apparatus. Even after he has won public office, continued party activity may be necessary to open up opportunities to run for higher office. The middle and upper leadership ranks of the American parties, for instance, have a goodly smattering of lawyers who seek a political career in a state legislature or the Congress and who would later gratefully accept a judgeship as a climax to their political career. Quite apart from party activity as a way of securing nominations, it is also an invaluable way of making the contacts, building the support, and raising the funds one needs to make the race for public office.

Patronage, preferment, and the political career all entail tangible rewards for the party worker, although the holding of public office may also bring non-tangible satisfactions. In addition, the party activist may work in the party to pursue the *economic rewards* of his own occupation or business. More than one American law practice has been founded with the contacts and publicity of political activity. Party contacts may also benefit the insurance and real-estate broker, or the small businessman or storekeeper. Or the partisan may, indeed, seek opportunities for vice or corruption. Considering both the understandable paucity of reliable information about it and the already low esteem in which the parties and their politicians are held, it is a subject one hesitates to broach. It seems beyond contest, however, that in a number of American communities power in the dominant party has been used to protect prostitution, gambling, or the rackets, or to extract protection money from local merchants and citizens. Among the politically cynical the over-all importance of these incentives has been comically overdrawn, but that exaggeration would hardly seem reason for pretending they do not exist at all.

Frequently overlooked in assessments of the incentives that bring men to the party are the whole congeries of *personal rewards* they find in service to the party. The party may promise upward social mobility, an opportunity to enter new social circles, or it may simply offer fellowship and friends for the lonely and a way of keeping busy for those on whom time hangs heavily. The "courthouse crowd" and the hangers-on at party headquarters testify to the potency of these social inducements. Involvement in the party may also offer a diversion and excitement the individual cannot find in his workaday life. The party stages great campaigns for great causes, engages the clever in a fascinating set of strategies, and brings them into the company of colorful and noted personalities. Politics is, as Frank Kent wrote, a "great game," an almost romantic escape from the frustration and drudgery of private life.

These personal rewards include the psychological as well as the social. Many middle-class Americans may be drawn to party service at least in part to satisfy an ingrained concept of civic duty and a nagging obligation to be concerned with public affairs. Party activity may, as Harold Lasswell has suggested, permit the activist to bolster his sagging self-esteem, offer him opportunities for manipulating others, or in other ways enable him to work out his adjustment needs. It may also afford an occasional outlet, sometimes even paranoid, for redress of real or imagined injury. It may permit the worker to identify himself with a powerful personality or to bask in the reflected status and esteem of the powerful. Or party service may simply puff the ego, as one observant commentator on American politics has suggested:

My guess is that people usually turn to politics for the same reason actors seek the stage. They need applause.

Like the theater, politics is a great nourisher of egos. It attracts men who are hungry for attention, for assurance that somebody loves them, for the soul-stirring music of their own voices. (Political speeches are not invariably made because the public craves wisdom, but oftener just because politicians love to talk — even when their only audience is other politicians. Note how hard it is for the chairman to throttle down the oratory at that lowliest of all political gatherings, the meeting of precinct leaders.) A main ingredient in the make-up of every successful politician is a thick slice of ham.

The enjoyment of the public stage may not explain the total political motives of all practitioners, but it contributes to the political incentive system of most of them. Without an ability to derive these personal satisfactions, indeed, politics as a vocation might well be intolerable.

Others may be attracted to work in the party by a desire to influence *policy making*. They may want to protect the interests of some group or interest in political life by either altering or maintaining public policy. They may seek government regulation of an industry or a segment of the trade-union movement, or they may want to intensify or buttress existing regulations. They may seek a general reduction of taxes or a reallocation of tax burdens, or an increase or decrease in particular expenditures. The policy aims may also be less material; racial equality, local civic reform, or a nuclear test ban may be powerful incentives. The increasing activity of interest group members in the parties indicates the attraction of this incentive. When organized labor urges its members to party activity, or the Chamber of Commerce urges businessmen, the purpose is at least partly to place in the parties men and women who will seek and elect candidates loyal to these interests.

Finally, the incentives of *ideology* recruit workers for the parties. In its fullest form it attracts men into a crusade for Marxism or democracy, for nationalism and national glory, for religious truth or virtue, or for racial equality or domination. More commonly in the American experience ideology involves more limited goals and values, many of which may be defined as policy alternatives. The messianic zeal of ideology often obscures the elements of personal interest and policy program at stake. Even the most grandiose social ideology offers, in addition to the power of the ideas themselves, immediate policy programs through which to reach its goals. Ideology, however, tends to be more concerned with the values and goals themselves and with the need for teaching and evangelizing for them. It rationalizes the pursuit of specific programs and policies as a more basic, longer-run, more highly integrated system of values. The abstract value has independent life and incentive force in itself. Within the American parties it may lure the liberal ideologue who is committed to a set of beliefs about equality in American society, about the responsibility and role of government, and about the dangers of unregulated economic power. This liberal ideology may persist beyond the success or failure of specific policy proposals, *e.g.*, for federal medical care to the aged or the taxation of business expense accounts. Not even policy success moots an ideology.

Any list such as this one, of course, reflects a number of arbitrary decisions. A number of other categories might have been used to group the various incentives. Clark and Wilson, for example, have proposed that the incentives to action within the party can be grouped into the material, the solidary, and the purposive. Furthermore, within any list there will be inevitable overlapping and indistinctness. The pursuit of public office and a political career may attract the young lawyer to party service, but that pursuit will probably also bring him direct economic gains and social and psychological satisfactions. These incentives may even be indistinct to the individual worker who comes to the party out of mixed motives, some or all of which he may not admit even to himself.

One final incentive remains — the secondary or reinforcing feelings of identification with or loyalty to the organization itself. Party members and workers may be attracted to the party for any number of reasons, but as they involve themselves even more in the party, they develop ties and loyalties to it, to its norms and goals, and to its leaders. The organization itself achieves a life and a value for them; it ceases to be merely an instrument for achieving their other incentives, becoming an end in itself. Its triumphs and losses themselves become issues. Identification with the party reinforces and perhaps even replaces the incentives that initially recruited the individual.

No party relies on a single incentive. Their incentives differ from one time and one area to another — from city to country, for instance — and they may differ from one level to another in the party hierarchy. Even within the same local party organization at one time the local patronage seeker may join the socially ambitious and the ideologically oriented. Given such a diversity of incentive one may well question the sweeping, universal theories of political motivation that would attribute it to a particular political personality, to a set of psychological needs, or to the monism of economic determinism. The varieties and shifts in party incentives suggest instead the truth of the old saw about politics and strange bedfellows.

THE ORGANIZATIONAL USES OF INCENTIVE

Individuals pursue their own aims and goals through work in the political party. The party "management," however, seeks to regulate and control the "payment" of the incentives in order to achieve the goals of the party. But not all incentives are equally useful in attracting party workers and contributors. Some will "purchase" qualitatively different forms of party work than others, and some are more easily manipulatable than others by party leadership.

The effectiveness and usefulness of the incentive depend, first of all, on the quantity and quality of the work it can induce. They depend, that is, on whether or not it will buy those things the party wants. If the party seeks continuous, year-round committee activity, the more tangible rewards are most likely to produce it. Incentives such as personal loyalty to a candidate or the social incentives produce more transitory and less intensive effort. Those incentives which will attract sign-posting or neighborhood canvassing are not likely to attract large contributors or hostesses for suburban coffee-klatch campaigning. In the long run the political party has to abandon those incentives in its control if they no longer attract the skills and commitments that the style of political competition and party organization demand.

Furthermore, the party must be able, if the incentive is to be useful to it, to control its granting in the first place. And the party cannot dangle the incentive without delivering and paying off at least part of the time. The enormous value of patronage as an incentive to the old-style political machines was in the power of the party to produce the jobs. So long as they could win elections (and they almost all dominated one-party cities) the patronage was theirs to dispense. But if the individual has been drawn to the party for some policy purpose, what assurance has he that the party can reward his efforts? He may find that the party lacks the immediate, monopolistic control over policy payoffs and that his chances of reward, given the inability of parties to discipline legislators and influence legislative policy making, might be greater if he were to switch his labors to an interest group. On the other hand, dominant parties in some state legislatures do exercise exactly that type of control over policy making in the states. And control over local city halls and courthouses may permit them to monopolize the granting of administrative privileges and preferments as well as formal changes in public policy.

Third, the value of an incentive increases to the party to the extent that it can be withdrawn and, therefore, used as a sanction or threatened sanction. Parties have long recognized that the power to give unaccompanied by the power to revoke diminishes sharply the usefulness of the incentive. The postmasterships covered after appointment by civil service tenure are an example. Generally the tangible rewards — the patronage job, the granting of the nod to seek public office, the administrative contract or preferment — can most easily be taken away. The party finds it difficult to allocate the ideological and policy incentives. So also the personal satisfactions are difficult to control. Any attempt to exclude the individual from the party group as a punishment may destroy also the social incentives of large numbers of other individuals and threaten the cohesion and solidarity of the local party.

Leadership within the parties often finds a whole array of administrative problems in the uses of the party's incentives. Often the goals of the party conflict. It may face the conflicting claims of the patronage-oriented party workers and those pursuing ideological incentives. That conflict breaks out over the selection of candidates to run on the party ticket. Is the party to support candidates with ideological commitments or those willing to provide the local patronage? During the 1930's Franklin Roosevelt used what remained of the shrinking federal patronage to build Congressional majorities for his legislative program rather than rebuild the state and local Democratic parties. His alternatives were either to use the patronage to extend the party's external appeal and satisfy the policy-oriented workers and voters — and this alternative he chose — or to reinvest the patronage into a program of attracting new workers into the local parties and expanding the total party work force. In the administration of its incentives the party faces difficult choices between rewarding:

1. one level or another of the party (the national-local dilemma)
2. one incentive or another (the patronage-seekers and the ideologues, for instance)
3. one service or another (the workers-contributors dilemma).

No administrative problem exceeds the danger that the rewards and incentives will become ends in themselves. The Republican party in the American South was for years run by patronage seekers who sought to keep the party small and exclusive so that the periodic Republican national patronage would not have to be parcelled out to a large number of people. Patronage and preferment rewards attract party workers and leaders who often care little if the party wins elections and new adherents so long as they take their cut of the spoils. In parties of ideology there is a similar danger in that the purity of the party gospel becomes an end in itself. Such an obsession with the rewards has dysfunctional consequences for the party in that its ability to contest elections and perform its other political functions is materially weakened.

In theory, of course, this perversion of party incentives ought not to occur. The party, in order to maintain its organizational health, has to replenish constantly the store of incentives it needs to purchase additional labor to produce its party functions. For the party to maintain its reward system and produce payoffs on it, it must win elections. But federalism enables the party to get its rewards from another level of party operation. Hence the Southern Republicans' ability to survive for many years on national Republican election victories. Local parties have also been able to garner those tangible rewards on occasion by collusive arrangements with the majority party. Unlike the operation of economic organizations, there is no one-to-one relation in the political party between the likelihood of receiving rewards and the quality or productiveness of work done in return. But for most parties the rewards do bear some relationship to the ability to win elections. Even those social and psychological rewards depend ultimately on the party's maintaining status, voter clientele, and the exhilaration of victory. Of all the incentives only those of ideology appear to be independent of electoral success. Small numbers of ideologues cling even in the United States to minor, non-competitive parties that have no prospect of winning elections. Some within the major parties feel similarly that they would gladly sacrifice victory to principle.

As long as it lasted, and for the type of party organization it augmented, patronage was almost the ideal incentive. Consider its advantages. Its lure was so great, especially in times and places of unemployment, that it produced continuous activity. The machine enjoyed complete control over it; the party could deliver the payoff with almost 100 per cent regularity, and it could in many cases freely revoke it. Patronage also brought with it other rewards for the recipient: a social mobility often denied him as a minority group member, the fellowship of party insiders, and the lordly satisfactions of helping local families in distress and need. For the party the patronage job not only rewarded a local worthy. If there were no legal or ethical restrictions, the party often "maced" the patronage payroll for compulsory party contributions. And if, as it often happened, the public duties of the appointee were not arduous, he could spend his days in the sweet service of the party. The public treasury thus provided the job for the worker, free labor for the party, and contributions for the party coffers. Through the charity of patronage the party was thrice blessed.

What happened, then, to patronage? It had never been without its disadvantages. Because most patronage jobs did not demand especially high skill or ability levels — no patronage system can by its definition expect widespread occupational expertise and experience — it recruited men whose political skills were also middling. That raised no problem as long as the work to be done was personal-contact work, canvassing, and rallying. But it failed to recruit the middle-class leadership that American politics increasingly needed after the 1920's. Furthermore, it attracted, again by its nature, leadership oriented to local politics and government, for the heart was where the patronage was. Finally, party workers attracted by the patronage often neglected the party functions of contesting elections, recruiting candidates, and propounding political programs. At the same time that patronage was thus declining in value to the party, it was being reduced in quantity by the spread of civil service and merit systems of public employment. To this day it remains a nice question whether reform is killing patronage or whether it is dying of natural political causes.

The incentives that replace patronage in the American parties do not permit the parties the degree of control and manipulation that patronage did. The new club movement builds on personal rewards and policy and ideological incentives. But these incentives are quite beyond the party's ability to control. Even should it dismiss or reject the partisan to deny him his rewards, he may find them in alliance with other political groups or organizations, such as, say, the Foreign Policy Association, the John Birch Society, or the League of Women Voters. Nor can the party easily control the payoffs; a thousand and one influences other than the party determine policy making in the Congress or a local city council. To be sure, these incentives attract workers and activists who relate to the personalities and issues of the day, who are oriented to the changing political functions of the party, and who have the skills and respectability the party needs. But their ties to the party are unilateral ones that they make and break. The party has the carrot, but not the stick, and other political organizations have carrots, too.

With the decline of the tangible incentives with which the parties maintained a continuing discipline and cohesion, they look anew to the secondary, reinforcing incentives of group solidarity and identification to carry the partisan along in loyal activity. Do

the new club parties, though, build these voluntary loyalties more
effectively than the classic party of patronage? March and Simon
suggest that the individual's identification with a group depends
on the prestige of the group, on the extent to which its goals are
seen as shared by the members, on the frequency of interactions
within the group, on the number of individual needs satisfied in it,
and on the minimization of competition between the individual
and members of the group. The case can be made that the club
type of party of reform as well as policy issues can maximize those
conditions. It is in many ways an attempt to recapture the group
solidarity and identification of the old-style party organization by
increasing the interactions of party workers and the number of
goals they might achieve in it. And compared to the older machine
it appears to be more successful in increasing the community prestige of the organization; it also reduces internal competitiveness
since workers do not have to compete for ideological and social incentives as they do for the few choice patronage plums and the
right to run for the few major elective offices.

The party is not, however, without means for building these
loyalties. It may foster solidarity by admitting party workers into
the decision-making processes of the party. Apart from the values
of rationality and responsibility it observes, intra-party democracy
may perform a useful function for the party as an organization.
Beyond these moves to solidarity the parties rely more and more
on the common set of policy and ideological goals to recruit
workers and to build organizational cohesion. In depending on
interest and ideology, however, the parties develop a party cadre
far more inclined to the politics of ideology than its electorate is.
Ultimately they have to reckon when ideological incentives for
the party workers will reach the point of diminishing returns —
the point at which they will purchase activity worth less than the
support of the voters they alienate.

SHAPERS OF INCENTIVES

To the first-generation son of Italian parents, ac-
tivity in the political party may offer social mobility and identification with a set of traditional American folkways. To his neighbor
it may offer adherence to a program of free-enterprise, laissez-faire

capitalism. Yet despite this diversity of incentives within the same party, all incentives are not equally available or valuable to it. The party operates in an incentive market economy in which forces often beyond its control influence both the supply of various incentives and the relative demand for them.

Unquestionably one of the most important factors determining the availability and value of incentives — their supply and the demand for them — is the political culture. It is the sum of the expectations, the goals, and the mores with which the public views and appraises the political system. It defines the customary, the expected, and the approved political activity. Some political cultures may accept the ethic of patronage, but others reject it for its violation of the values of non-partisanship, expertise, and experience in public office. An increasingly middle-class American political culture, by looking with disfavor on the rewards of patronage and preference, has accelerated those reform movements which preach their elimination. So also has it demeaned the prestige and status of the patronage job. Similarly, the American political culture discounts the prestige of many elective positions, making the pursuit of an elective political career less attractive than it would be in Great Britain or the new African states.

More general social and economic conditions may also shape the outlines and designs of the incentive system. Increasing reliance on policy and ideological incentives within the American parties reflects some of them; increasing education, political communication, and political awareness are necessary conditions for the creation of those incentives. Or to take another illustration: where class lines are tightly drawn and opportunity for social mobility is limited, the value of the party as a vehicle of social mobility will increase. General economic conditions of full employment opportunities in the private sector of the economy diminish the value of the political job, whereas severe unemployment enhances it. Even the social structure of the community affects the supply and demand of party incentives. Chroniclers of the new club movement in American politics have noted that its development, strongly supported by the personal incentives, has been greatest in urban centers in which friendless, shifting populations and rootless new arrivals seek a congenial social circle.

Finally, the political system itself shapes the patterns of rewards. A whole pattern of local government reforms — the city manager, local civil service, nonpartisan elections, and the instruments of direct democracy — had as one of its main goals the minimization of party control of legislative policy making and administrative discretion. Federalism, too, both multiplies and disperses the rewards of elective and appointive office. The long ballot, to take another illustration, means in many American localities that there is a large list of paid public positions in which the parties, by controlling the elective processes, place their deserving aspirants. The dictates of Jacksonian democracy have, in general, worked to supply the parties with a plenitude of tangible incentives. Finally, the outlines of political controversy and debate dictate the availability of incentives. For the ideologically inclined, Stimson Bullitt writes:

> Politics offers more incentive when goals of policy can be seen and are approached. The periods of consolidation tend to be less tempting than the periods of advance.

Though American politics in the 1930's debated great issues and matters of policy, the politics of the 1950's and 1960's have been those of consolidation and time-marking. The consequent withdrawal of ideological rewards has alienated the more vigorous activists of both the left and the right.

The supply of incentives on which any party draws is defined basically by three factors:

   1. The availability of the incentive.
   2. The demand for the incentive by the politically active individual.
   3. The pattern of needs of the party (*i.e.*, their functions and the ways in which they are carried out).

The decline of the importance of patronage, which we discussed earlier, illustrates the impact of all three. The third factor, however, is less clear and obvious, because it is both cause and result of the pattern of incentives. New demands in the American society for middle-class parties and for more attention to policy and ideology have forced the parties to look for men and skills that the traditional patronage posts cannot attract. On the other hand, party organization and style may be largely a reflection of the men and skills the available incentives recruit. Indeed, the inability of political incentives today to "buy" a quantity of political effort equal to that of a generation or two ago has forced upon the American parties new forms of organization and new patterns of political activities.

Recent trends in the incentive patterns of the American parties amply illustrate the impact of changes in incentives on the parties themselves. One consequence of the shift away from patronage and preferment has been a growing worker participation and influence in the affairs of the party. Patronage and preference could be dispensed and manipulated apart from the electoral and other political functions of the party. The party worker often cared little about the running of the party as long as his immediate rewards were forthcoming. Such a clear division between political management and labor breaks down as the party shifts to incentives of policy and ideology. They involve the work and functions of the party; their recruitees care deeply about and want to influence the management of the party. The achievement of the goals of policy and ideology depend directly on how the party carries out its educational function, its electoral function, and its supervision and control of governmental power. Except for the necessity to win to keep the jobs available, the patronage system was discrete from the guidance of the party in its political functions. The two worlds of party operation are joined when the party shifts to a politics of policy and ideology. In fact, as the activists satisfy their ideological urges in the selection of compatible candidates and the statement of explicit programs and principles, they may frighten the party electorate and compromise the electing function. That, to repeat an illustration, is increasingly the dilemma of the Republican-party conservatives in the 1960's.

These changes would also indicate a greater emphasis on either a more widely shared decision-making process within the party or a need for party leadership to consider the party workers as a clientele as much in need of wooing as the party's voters. Now less able to depend on punishments and sanctions, the American party is being forced to depend more on the solidarity of common policy goals and experience or a more general group iden-

tification. The authoritarian, hierarchical style of the political
machine — the kernel of truth in the exaggerated image of the
omnipotent boss and the edicts of the smoke-filled rooms — un-
dermines the solidarity goals, and one finds less and less of it. The
price of this change may be a decline in the effectiveness of party
decision making. Haggling, deadlock public shows of party disunity may result, and have resulted, and it becomes more and
more difficult for the parties to make key decisions. The bargaining and balancing of utilities involved in drafting a representative party slate of candidates can be done far more easily in the
small room than it can be done in the deliberative convention.

The American parties are now facing a series of problems that
grow out of the heterogeneity of incentives on which they must
rely. Patronage and preference exist side-by-side with ideology
and policy, political career along with personal rewards and satisfactions. The battle of the Tammany organization in New York
with the new reform parties has its less dramatic and less clear-cut
parallels all over the country. The conflict is really many conflicts.
The leadership of Tammany clings to the tangible incentives; the
new reform organizations have chosen those of policy and ideology. Their disagreements begin there with one side's attacks on
the ethics of patronage and preferment, and epithets of "egghead"
and "do-gooder" from the other. Their frequently conflicting goals
also lead them to conflicts over candidates and platforms, and over,
indeed, every facet of party operation. The older syndrome of incentives, furthermore, focuses attention on local politics; it is there
that the remaining patronage and preferment exist and where en-
try to a political career always existed. The new incentives of policy and ideology tend, as policy making centralizes, to focus on
state and national politics. The possibilities for conflict multiply
again. Finally, the two sets of incentives attract men of sharply
differing political styles, different education and social status, and
entirely different ways of life. They are at best uncomfortable
with each other; at worst they are deeply suspicious.

And so the incentives on which the party depends provide a useful clue to many other aspects of its operations and structure. The
organization, the leadership, and the activities of the party depend

to some extent on the unifying, solidifying, and recruiting powers of the system of rewards and sanctions. The nature and quality of the parties' products reflect in significant ways the kinds of political currency with which they recruit their labor.

6

The contest
for office

In November of 1962 Robert Taft, Jr. won
election as Ohio's congressman-at-large in an overwhelming landslide. The victory was not unexpected, however, and the reason
extended beyond Congressman Taft's personal qualifications and
distinguished political name. His opponent, Richard D. Kennedy,
a 39-year-old Clevelander running on a segregationist platform,
had been disowned by the Democratic party after winning the
May primary. In that primary most of the large county Democratic organizations and Democratic leaders had supported a Cin-
cinnati councilman, John J. Gilligan, over the other ten contestants. But in a state-wide contest in which no candidate was
known beyond his own area of the state and in which eleven
candidates divided the vote, the magic name of Kennedy had
brought the winner 20 per cent of the votes cast and a margin
of 2500 votes over Gilligan. A shocked Democratic organization
refused to support him in the general election, and Governor
Michael DiSalle announced that he would not vote for him. The
election was left virtually by default to Taft.

The nightmare that happened to the Ohio Democratic party in 1962 happens to few party organizations in the United States, but it haunts many of them. In failing to control a state-wide primary election, the party surrendered its chances to win the general election. But worse yet, it suffered the humiliation of having to repudiate the candidate in order not to endanger further the other candidates on the party ticket. The embarrassment of the Ohio Democrats highlights the importance of the nomination to the party's electing function. Too often the dramatic, well-publicized events of the election campaign obscure the fact that the truly meaningful choices of candidates have often taken place months earlier in the primary election or, even before that, in the party's pre-primary maneuverings to organize party support for a single would-be primary candidate. The temptation is very great, as a result, to overemphasize the role of the party in the election campaign and to undervalue its control — and especially its need to control — the nomination.

Political parties as completely caught up in the electoral function as the American parties flourish only if they win elections. A competitive electoral party depends heavily on the material and psychological rewards of success at the polls. The recruitment of capable and attractive candidates, the single most important ingredient of the party's public image, depends on favorable prospects for victory. Rewards for the party's workers, whether they are a patronage job or the enactment of public policy, depend on the party's periodic victories. Even the social and personal rewards are hard to come by in the demoralized minority party. Electoral parties find that in politics, as in business and war, nothing succeeds quite like success. The competitive party attracts candidates and workers whose status and acceptability in the community transfer to the party itself.

THE CRUCIAL NOMINATING STEP

Viewed realistically, the party's election activities begin with its attempts to groom possible candidates for the future, continue with elaborate prenomination procedures for sifting out potential candidates, progress through the actual nomination of the candidate, and conclude with the general election campaign. The election of an American President, especially for the losing party, is in this sense a four-year process that begins with the post-mortems of party spokesmen the day after the preceding election.

To this lengthy chain of elective activities the nominating step and all that precedes it is the key. Loss of control of the nomination poses a series of the gravest threats to the party. The party's candidates bear the party label, and they are its public representatives. Parties will be known by the inept, unqualified, and venal candidates they present. They, too, may want to use public offices as rewards for party service, but they can do so only by controlling nomination to them. Should the party want to hold its candidates to the pledges of its platform — whether by gratitude to the party, fear of its disfavor in future elections, or a personal acceptance of the party's position — it can do so only if it controls the nomination of candidates. Finally, failure to nominate means that the party cannot organize a balanced ticket of candidates with suitable representatives on it of important ethnic, religious, and regional groups. Indeed, so crucial is the control of nominations to the political party that the surest sign of factionalism in the party is a persistent split over the choice of candidates.

The nominating steps, of course, assume an even greater significance in areas of one-party domination. Here the men nominated by the dominant party will almost surely be elected. Dazzled by an over-all national party competitiveness that measures an electoral margin of 10 or 15 per cent as a landslide, we tend to overestimate the local competitiveness of the two parties. From 1956 through 1962 between 56 and 62 per cent of the members of the American House of Representatives won their seats by margins of more than 20 per cent over their nearest competitor. The cumulative competitiveness of the British parliamentary candidates also conceals many areas of one-party dominance. In the British general election of 1959, for instance, close to one-half (298 of 630, or 47.3 per cent) of the candidates elected to Commons won by the same 20 per cent margin.

For most of the political parties of the Western democracies the control of nominations poses no severe problem. The party's executive committee, a special candidate screening or selection committee, or a self-appointed group of party leaders bears the bulk of the selection responsibility. Often they also seek a *pro forma* ratification by the party membership. In a few instances broadly representative party organs such as conferences or conventions make the nominations. In any event, the selection of candidates is viewed as a matter of internal party business. The American parties, however, must nominate within the unique and peculiar limits of the direct primary, a device through which its framers intended to deny the leadership and cadres of the American parties that power to nominate. Only the nomination of the American Presidential candidates and a few state offices have escaped this transfer of the nominating power from the party's workers and leaders to its electorate. In its most expansive form, the open primary, the direct primary even permits the members and identifiers of the other party to wander into the party's nominating processes in search of electoral excitement.

Viewed historically, the direct primary is a recognition that brokerage, electoral parties act responsively as nominators only when other competitive parties threaten them. By the beginning of the 20th century many sectors of the country had drifted into one-partyism. Within these dominant parties powerful leaders and caucuses, usually fully aware of their monopolistic power, nominated ruthlessly and often in disregard of their electorates. Candidates of meager abilities and complete subservience to the party often resulted. If there were no competitive party system to control the monopolistic nominators, then public policy would. What antitrust legislation was to the corporate monopolists, the direct primary was to the single, dominant party.

By opening the nomination of party standard-bearers to a broad and often undefined party clientele, the direct primary threatens the party in three crucial ways. First, it weakens party control over nominations, with the possible results of candidates disloyal to the party, candidates without good electoral prospects, and the poorly balanced ticket. Often the candidate best able to win in a primary election dominated by small numbers of motivated partisans is not the candidate best calculated to make a broad appeal to the general electorate. Second, since the candidate may pass the independent test of the primary on his own, he may feel and express little debt to the party. Should he be elected, the party may find him uncooperative on patronage matters or unresponsive to party urgings on program and policy. If the legislator can win nomination without party help, or despite its opposition, he has robbed the party of its most powerful sanction over him. Third, the direct primary is the most powerful divisive force within the American parties. Primaries often pit party leader against party leader, party voters against party voters, often opening deep and unhealing party wounds. They also dissipate party financial and personnel resources. Party leadership usually finds that it has no choice but to take sides in a primary battle, the alternative being the possible triumph of the weaker candidate.

The American parties, although seriously discommoded by the primary, have developed skills for managing it. Generally the party would prefer that its anointed candidate run unopposed in the primary, but that requires the party to move swiftly and effectively. Some party group or endorsing convention must decide in favor of a candidate and persuade him to enter the primary. Perhaps the party has groomed a candidate for months or years, or perhaps it has promised the chance to run in return for a candidate's bowing out of an earlier primary. At the same time party leadership may be working to discourage other potential candidates, cajoling them with promises of future support or threatening them with loss of party favor and a blighted political career. Ideally these missions should be accomplished before the first filing date for primary candidates so that unauthorized candidates will be forewarned of the party's decision. If its efforts to prevent primary competition have been unavailing, it turns then to contest the primary. If it cannot control the candidates, it may control the voters. Its organizational and financial assets help to support the chosen candidate and mobilize support for him.

Basically, one factor above all others — the general apathy of voters in primaries — eases the party's task in primary battles. The voters most apt to vote are those most loyal to the party and its choices. With primary turnouts often no larger than from 30 to 50 per cent of the electorate, a small and tightly disciplined band of voters can carry an election. Much of the party's campaign in a primary contest aims at a selective stimulation of that part of the electorate most likely to respond to its cues. If, aided by general voter apathy, it can control both the size and the composition of the turnout, its prospects of success are good. This is probably the greatest reason why the parties tend to discourage general "get out the vote" campaigns at the primaries. If a given ward in an American city has 10,000 registered voters, about 5000 of these might be expected to vote in party A's primary. But with primary turnouts at about 40 per cent, only 2000 will. In a primary contest 1000 votes will win. If there are three or four more candidates to distract uninformed and undisciplined voters — and some parties have not been above inveigling "dummy" candidates into primary races for just that purpose — some 600 or 700 voters might suffice to carry the primary.

The parties themselves, however, often overlook one other consequence of the primary, the impetus it gives to party decentralization. That consequence may in the long run be the most important one, for although the parties can bypass its limits on their nominating power, it is hard to imagine how its decentralizing effects can be neutralized. American political leaders who happened to notice press reports of the Indian Congress party's purge of its members of parliament in 1957 must have read in utter disbelief. In order to recast the party's image and meet criticisms of its aging leadership, the national Parliamentary Board, the party agency that selects and approves candidates for local constituencies, dropped almost one-third of the party's incumbent members of Parliament. Such centralized nominating is rare, but other parties such as those of the British maintain a central clearance over local constituency nominations, a power they use more as a threat in preliminary negotiations than as a sanction. Central party headquarters in Great Britain also promotes the candidacies of promising young men in the party by spotting them in likely constituencies. Even such central control as this is unthinkable in the United States. Political culture and tradition work against it, but even were they overcome, the primary election remains a barrier to centralized nominating. No national clearance of candidates or attempts to remove disloyal or ineffective incumbents can avail so long as the candidate can win a primary. And outside intervention in a direct primary is a far riskier matter than pressure on local party leadership. Franklin Roosevelt in 1938 urged the primary defeats of a number of conservative Democratic senators and representatives. The voters of all but one of the constituencies administered what was probably his most humiliating political defeat.

Not all of the party's nomination failures can, however, be blamed on the direct primary. Other factors must explain why American parties, all of which work under the primary, differ so greatly in their role and their success in controlling nominations. The party's own lackluster indifference and organizational unreadiness may be the cause. It may simply lack the strength, the interest, and the know-how to manage the primary. The incumbent officeholder also limits the party's nominating power. Even if the party is dissatisfied with his performance, it usually concedes him the nomination. His period in office, and all of its advantages and opportunities for service and contacts in the constituency, enables the average officeholder to free himself from party control by building broad and independent sources of political power. He may also use his prestige and office to increase his influence within the party. Furthermore, the constituency's political culture may value political independence and exalt the insurgent. If it resents party "bossism" and "dictatorship," it may curtail party activity in the primary. The effective management of the primary that voters in New York, Philadelphia, and Chicago accept as a matter of course would outrage the political sensitivities of people in many parts of the United States. Finally, the parties may, in order to propitiate blocs of voters or to keep contributors pleased, voluntarily share the nominating power with private groups. Business or labor groups, for instance, may impose a veto power or their own chosen candidates as a price of their continued support.

THE PRESIDENCY AND CONVENTION NOMINATIONS

The convention system of nominating candidates is everywhere in flight in the United States, except in the nomination of candidates for the one pair of offices in the national constituency. The processes by which we choose Presidential and

Vice-Presidential candidates remain the great exception to the primary system, through which we nominate virtually all other office-seekers in the country (Table 6-1). The great quadrennial nominating conventions, half carnival and half revival meeting, in which Presidents are picked remain as the last vestiges of a system of party controlled nominations that endured well into this century.

Table 6-1 STEPS IN THE NOMINATION PROCESS

	Prenomination	*Nomination*	*Election*
Presidential elections	Selection of delegates by convention or Presidential primary	Convention	Electoral college; election by plurality within states and majority of votes in college
Almost all other American elections	Placement on Primary ballot by petition or convention	Primary election, and a few conventions	Plurality vote at general election

The Presidential nominating conventions stand in the American party system as the single manifestation of the national parties. Their few days of operation is the only period within the four-year cycle of American politics in which a national party might truly be said to exist. The convention celebrates the saints and symbols of the nebulous national party in a pageant of unity and solidarity. Yet the persistent localism and decentralization of the parties obtrude on even this brief hour of the national party. The delegations from the states come to choose a pair of potential winners for the national party, but they come as well to work out local purposes and goals. The conventions have often had to settle contests for control of state organizations. The state delegations also engage in the bargaining of the convention for local purposes: to secure the Vice-Presidential nomination or a cabinet seat for a local political personage or to win concessions on a plank in the party platform. And as they choose a national ticket they cannot fail to ask what its impact will be on the state ticket. Several state delegations with Roman Catholic candidates for state-wide office in 1960 hesitated to support Senator Kennedy's candidacy out of a concern about the total impact of a number of Catholics on the ballot in their states.

Convention or no, the direct primary has found its way into Presidential nominating politics, although in an unusual role. In less than one-third of the states delegates to the national conventions are chosen in varying types of Presidential primaries. Most of these primaries also offer the voter some way by which he can register his preference among those who seek his party's Presidential nomination. These primaries, then, are in the nature of prenomination instruments for choosing and instructing the party's nominators. The parties' brief against them is extensive: they are costly, they put the candidates through a grueling series of jousts, they extend the effective period of a Presidential campaign to nine months, they handicap the candidate with limited resources, and they ignore the lesser-known men of the party. Above all, they deprive the convention of its flexibility in choosing a candidate who can unite the party as well as win the Presidency.

In general the Presidential nominating conventions do not fare well in public esteem these days. The supporters of disappointed aspirants resent the power of the party cadre as "kingmakers" at the conventions. The television audience finds them long, prolix, and disorganized, and the impression abounds during them that sheer boredom will kill the American parties. There have even been proposals to abolish the conventions and replace them with national nominating primaries. But the parties have heard and resisted these criticisms before. More disturbing to them is the possibility that the national conventions are losing their control of the nomination of the candidates. Preconvention campaigns, aimed at committing large numbers of delegates, have been growing in scope and effectiveness. They reached something of a zenith in the Kennedy campaign of 1959 and 1960 to win delegate support in primaries, state conventions, and conversations and bargains with influential state leaders. Accompanying that tactic was another campaign in the media to publicize the Kennedy name, face, and family. As a preconvention campaign it set new standards for sheer organization, integrated strategy, and over-powering resources.

Any threat to the nominating conventions, whether a threat of replacement by a single national primary, or one of diminishing effectiveness, forces one to consider their place in the party system. In the nominating convention the political party, to the extent it controls the nomination process, also performs the vital rites of party integration. Factions and viewpoints within the party are reconciled and compromised, and their differences are submerged in the convention's wash of enthusiasm. A new harmony within the party follows the catharsis of combat. At a convention the party can carefully balance, in its selection of candidates and the adoption of a platform, the needs for external appeal to the electorate with those internal needs for organizational cohesion and enthusiasm. It has long been the parties' contention that the direct primary does not enable them to perform that integrative function, and that it instead opens new conflicts and new differences within the party without providing processes for their resolution. The party is left with no occasion on which it can awaken old organizational loyalties, resolve its differences, and gird itself for the general election battle.

The making of nominations is the one political decision the American party makes as a political organization. The electorate decides the general election. If one deprives the party organization of the power to nominate, the party is deprived of one of its few *raisons d'être* as a political party. Ultimately, the organization, stripped of one of its most meaningful tasks, will be weakened. V. O. Key has suggested that the onset of the direct primary in the United States has resulted in an atrophy of party organization for exactly that reason. It is also on this ground and because of the needs for party integration that the case for the convention system of Presidential nominations rests. One need not, of course, make an all-or-nothing argument for the nominating convention. As an integrative device it is organizationally necessary the larger the party, the less frequent its other associations, the more heterogeneous its composition, and the greater its internal policy and ideological differences. Unquestionably the nominating convention serves a far more vital organizational function for the ephemeral national party organizations of the American parties than it did for the city machine.

THE ART AND CRAFT OF CAMPAIGNS

The American parties have been struggling for 50 years to control the nomination of candidates for office. At the same time they have had to undertake a second fight to maintain their influence in the general election campaign. No political institutions guarantee the American parties any major part in that campaign. Proportional representation systems that use the party lists force the candidates to subordinate their campaign to the party's, since the voters elect a party list rather than individual candidates. Similarly, since the ultimate selection of the cabinet and the prime minister in parliamentary systems depends on party majorities, voters in local parliamentary elections know that they are supporting a party bid for governmental power when they choose candidates. Within the American political system, on the other hand, institutional elements such as the separation of powers and the many non-partisan elections undermine rather than support the party's campaign role.

Party control over campaigns flourishes where the party organization itself remains the most important campaign device. Where the hordes of committeemen and their regular canvassing and contacts with voters produce a cohesive vote for the straight party ticket, the party dominates the election by its indispensability as the chief campaign weapon. However, as the style of American campaigns turns to the mass media, to radio and television speeches and "great debates," and to the arts of advertising and public relations, the political party no longer plays the main role as the organizing intermediary in the campaign. Candidates increasingly mobilize their own electorates. The "pros" within the American parties formerly were the crafty, experienced "pols," the committeemen and local leaders of the party cadre. A new elite of professionals — the statisticians, the pollsters, the research analysts, the media and advertising men — are replacing them. The parties rely less on the folk wisdom of the old pros and more on the costly, prestigeful science of the new ones. The party used to rely implicitly on workers' reports on matters such as the acceptability of possible candidates to the voters of the locality. Today it may well test the voter sentiment with a pre-primary opinion survey.

The impact of these shifts has been twofold. The political party has not pre-empted or monopolized the services and campaign know-how of the new pros. Most of it has developed outside of regular party channels, and, unlike the old folk wisdom and expertise, it is available outside the party to any candidate or group that can meet its substantial price. The parties find themselves technologically replaced as campaign instruments by new kinds of knowledge and by its open availability. Second, the new expertise of the media experts raises the costs of campaigning substantially. Much of the old-time organization work came free to the party, in time exchanged for the many rewards it gave for service. Not so the new science of politics. Its expensiveness forces the local party to seek candidates of means, the help of non-party groups — organized labor provided the Louis Harris polling services to local Democratic organizations in 1962 — or the help of central party campaign funds. Whichever alternative it chooses, the local party suffers a decline in its campaign role.

This shift in campaigning, with its attendant changes in party skills and personnel, may also be viewed as a shift to the candidate-centered campaign. Within the American parties the day seems to be gone when a Presidential candidate can run a passive campaign such as Warren G. Harding's 1920 siege of the front porch. The campaign has increasingly become a testing of the candidate, a challenge to his ability to establish rapport with the electorate and to face the rigors, the crises, and the surprises of the campaign. The candidate relies on those arts and techniques which will bring him or his public presence directly to his voting supporters. He may use his party tie only as a supporting, auxiliary identification, or, indeed, he may ignore it should he think his personal appeal stronger without it. The new campaign style is, indeed, merely another aspect of the trend to personalism and mass leadership in democratic politics over the world in this century.

Despite over-all trends in the nature of American political campaigns, there remains room for a vast variety of party campaign roles in the American political system. The American federal system has permitted the creation of an enormous number of public offices, most of them with short terms. The sheer volume of recruiting, nominating, and campaigning that results from the total number of elections contributes to decentralization and local autonomy in the parties' nominating and electing tasks. The infinite variety of local conditions and clienteles as well as the sheer number of selections and campaigns are probably beyond the competence and mastery of any national party organ. Where central party organizations have controlled local nominations and elections, they have never had to cope with the sheer quantity of the American system.

From this decentralization there flows a torrent of troubles for the parties in the campaigns. The multiplicity of elections may be well beyond the power of the casual local party to contest. The endemic difficulty that minority parties have in filling the party ticket illustrates that problem. Special ad hoc campaign organizations spring up to manage a specific campaign, capitalize on a local issue, or bypass an unpopular or inept local party organization. Organizations of volunteers for candidates represent hostages to local political cultures of independence and party hostility. And state party organizations may choose not to support the national Presidential ticket; some, such as Senator Byrd's in Virginia in 1952, may even support the candidate of the other party. In this chaos of campaign decentralization and concessions to local conditions, the parties find an almost infinite number of relationships to the campaigns of their candidates.

A thousand and one institutional details in the American political system also limit and confuse the roles of the parties in the campaigns. Non-partisan elections impose obvious restrictions. Two other illustrations should suffice. The regulation of campaign contributions and expenses in many states also encourages the fragmentation of campaigns and campaign organization. Sharp limits on expenditures by the parties and the candidate have promoted the creation of temporary, voluntary campaign organizations that help spread out the receipt and expenditure of funds. Finally, Americans rarely realize also how the fixed dates of their elections minimize party power in the campaigns. In Great Britain and other parliamentary systems the prime minister and cabinet often schedule elections unexpectedly and on short notice, leaving the candidates little time to prepare for a campaign of only about a month's duration. A persistent, well-organized, and fully mobilized party in such an electoral system has no competitor as an effective campaign organizer. The American candidate, on the other hand, has a longer and predictable period of time in which to popularize himself and in which to recruit and organize an *ad hoc* campaign organization.

While the party operates externally as a campaign organization, it is also at work in the cognitive systems of large numbers of voters during the campaign. Voters in India, large numbers of whom are illiterate, vote by recognizable symbol: the cow for one party, the star for another, the sheaf of grain for a third. The easily identifiable party symbol leads the illiterate voter to the candidate of his choice. But what is literally true in India may figuratively be true in the Western democracies. The party loyalties of the individual voter often lead him to a candidate and dominate his voting decision. His loyalties to a party may override his loyalties to a candidate, or may dictate to him a preference for one candidate.

Voting the straight ticket in a number of elections, however, need not necessarily result from party attachments. A voter may consistently choose the candidates of one party because it is the only party with any real chance of winning, because he finds its candidates consistently more appealing, or because of the attractiveness of policies to which the party has attached itself. Consistency in voting for the candidates of one party may cover the operation of other factors affecting the voting decision. Only some independent measure of party loyalty or identification can cut the tangle of influences. The survey data of the Survey Research Center's *American Voter* provide the measures of that identification in the form of the voters' description of themselves as "strong" or "weak" members of one of the parties or as "independents."

Although it represents the most enduring loyalty affecting the voting decision, the cognitive "party" will not automatically carry greater weight than other influences in a given choice or election. The Survey Research Center's study of the 1952 Presidential election indicates a general preference of the electorate, *ceteris paribus*, for the Democratic party. Yet, a compelling candidate, Dwight D. Eisenhower, aided by the issue of a lingering and vexing war in Korea, overcame that pull of party loyalties. A sizable national majority of Americans in this generation have repeatedly expressed that preference for the Democratic party, and yet the party has not monopolized the national elections. Other appeals — reactions toward candidates, attitudes on policy issues, and group-related loyalties — have been at work. A goodly portion of campaign strategy involves attempts at a differential and selective playing on these various appeals. The campaign should reinforce those voters for whom the party is a major political reference group, but for those segments of the population less inclined to party, it must emphasize the party's program or the appeal and attractiveness of its candidates.

The fables and myths of "good citizenship" have long celebrated that voter, the independent, who has freed himself from these party attachments and who makes his electoral choice unhampered by any long-run political loyalties. As the man of lightest party attachments, he is presumably the emancipated and rational political man. That civic ideal reveals, of course, much of the anti-party bias of the middle-class American political culture. The data of the SRC, however, suggest that the stereotype of the independent must be modified. The self-described independents tend to be less attentive, less informed, and less interested about politics than do the voters of stronger party preference. Furthermore, independents within the American electorate of the 1950's had not cast off the influence of party. Both in 1952 and 1956 the independents voted more than two to one for Eisenhower and, more important, displayed pro-Republican perceptions of certain policy issues, of the two candidates, and of the general issue of the role of government.

While party as a political organization is organizing the campaign in the real political world, party as a personal loyalty organizes the political world of the individual citizen. As the authors of the *American Voter* write:

If some voters respond directly to a lasting sense of party identification, the behavior of most of the electorate is better explained as a response to current evaluations of what they are acting toward. We have conceived these evaluations as a field of attitude forces whose strength and direction and mutual consistency determine behavior in an immediate sense. The role of party identification seems primarily to be that of an antecedent factor that colors these attitudes as they are formed. By no means is party the only antecedent: this field of psychological forces reflects the influence of a great range of prior factors, which may at times lead the individual to form attitudes inconsistent with his stable party attachment. But the role of general partisan orientations in molding attitudes toward the elements of politics is very clear.

The party as a cognitive reality selects the elements of political reality most congenial to it and gives structure and stability to the individual's political cosmos. The political campaign and the party's part in it, therefore, progress on parallel levels — in the world of external events and in the cognitive perceptions of the electorate. Ideally, the party would like the two levels to converge before election day.

THE MYTH OF PARTY MONOPOLY

Nothing so marks the strong party as its ability to pick men, run them in a primary without competition, and elect them to office. From that control of the nomination and election processes flows the other power of holding office holders responsible, in debt and discipline, to a party program. The locus of the nominating power within the party probably affords the best single index to the general locus of power in the party. The highly centralized parties control, at least in part, even local nominations. Whoever in the party effectively sets the criteria for the candidates of the electoral party is, in the long run, making the most important decisions for it. Within many American parties it is the candidates and officeholders themselves who control the nomination-election process. They frequently dominate the leadership of the party and often make of it little more than a formalized vehicle for their re-election campaigns. Possibly, in a party system as exclusively committed to the electoral function as the

American, it is inevitable that the party leadership will be dominated by the seekers of public office. Their incentives for political action and the party's major task are one.

Generalizations about the roles of the American parties in nominating and electing candidates are difficult to make. They range from vigor and strength to inertia and impotence, but in all events the decentralization of the process leaves the responsibility to the local party organization. Any number of factors limit the ability of the party to control the process — the direct primary, the political culture and expectations of an electorate suspicious of party strength, the limitations of the party organization and its expectations for itself, external events in the American society such as wars and depressions, and institutional facts such as non-partisanship, to mention some of the more important ones.

The popular American solution to the dilemmas of unravelling and describing the specific role of the party in the nomination and election of candidates has been to overestimate it uncritically. It is a part of the conventional wisdom of American politics to assume that, since the parties are electoral parties, they dominate and monopolize the contesting of elections. Several generations of party histories have been told as if they were the history of American elections, the assumption apparently being that the victories of a party's candidates tell us something about the party. Similarly, the myths of the party professional include one that attributes all electoral outcomes to either the successes or the failures of the party organization. The party's role in the election process, they seem to argue, is only a matter of skill, effort, and willpower. The conventional wisdom, however, overestimates both the party's role in the American election and its freedom to shape its own role in the electoral process. The myth overestimates the degree to which the party monopolizes and controls the processes for selecting public officials. When the party cannot assert that control the fault appears to be the party's, the result of its lassitude, inertia, or ineptness. There are, however, genuine limits to the role even an electoral party can play in electing candidates. All possible party effort will not sweep aside the limits of a political culture that cherishes the belief that primary elections ought to remain free of party discipline and control.

That the American parties do not monopolize the function of organizing majorities behind candidates in the American political system is obvious. The reasons have in part been suggested in this chapter. To describe the difficulties the parties have in asserting their classic function is not, however, to deny their superiority to other political organizations in performing it. The effectiveness of the political party as an elector can best be described by ticking off the latent functions it performs for a democracy by its electoral function. The election is the occasion for its recruitment of political leadership. In that recruitment the parties have at times undeniably set less than acceptable standards by putting party loyalty or political worthiness above all other criteria. But whatever the shortcomings of the party as a responsible recruitment agency, it is preferable to the less open and less public recruitment and criteria of non-party groups. When all agencies of recruitment abdicate, the candidates in effect recruit themselves, leaving only the essentially uninformed voters to judge their ambitions and qualifications.

Nor can the parties perform their other latent functions in the democracy if they cannot perform their electing function. Because the party embraces larger aggregates of voters, it is most capable of compromising political differences as it organizes majorities. It is better able to simplify and codify political choices, to align them behind stable interests and symbols. Furthermore, the parties add an essential element of drama and excitement to the often drab world of public affairs. For most citizens, busy with their personal problems and their immediate environment, the affairs of government and the management of the democracy seem remote, forbidding, and even esoteric. The parties recast that political system into a picture of elemental conflict, and their leaders personalize and symbolize the great choices and alternatives available. They are, in brief, publicists and organizers of the democratic political processes in a way that none of their competitors has ever matched.

7

The party
and the uses of power

IN MAY OF 1945 Winston Churchill, then Prime
Minister of Great Britain, prepared to lead a British delegation
to the conference of the Allies at Potsdam, Germany. Since the
conference was to open after polling day in the July general
election, but before the announcement of the results, he invited
Clement Attlee and Ernest Bevin, the Labour Party's leaders, to
accompany him. Harold Laski, the chairman of Labour's National
Executive Committee, issued a statement asserting that Attlee
could attend only as an observer, since neither the party executive
nor the Parliamentary Labour Party had met to advise and instruct him on the issues that would be discussed at Potsdam. In
the exchange between Churchill and Attlee that followed, the
Prime Minister observed that the Labour Party constitution apparently permitted the executive council to advise, instruct, and
hold responsible a Labour Prime Minister. He might have added
that such an expectation was an old article of faith for many
Labourites. Mr. Attlee, however, replied that the National Executive Council had a right to be consulted but that it had no power

to challenge the policies and conduct of a Labour Prime Minister.

During the same years, the middle and late 1940's, the Committee on Political Parties of the American Political Science Association surveyed the relationship between the parties and policy making in the United States and found it wanting. Unlike Mr. Churchill's fears of party domination of the legislative party and legislative leadership, the American scholars deplored its absence in the American political system. The major American parties, the committee charged, were incapable of stating coherent party programs, electing candidates pledged to them, and ultimately ensuring that those programs would be enacted into public policy. They failed to meet the standards of the "responsible" party because they were unable to generate sufficient party discipline to hold their elected candidates responsible both to a party program and through it to the men and women who voted for it. Even though the committee's report, appropriately entitled *Toward a More Responsible Two-Party System,* received something less than unanimous acclaim from the committee's academic colleagues, it has in the years since its issuance set the pattern for a fruitful evaluation of the role and performance of the American parties.

These two events reflect in their contrasting ways the single persistent issue of the responsibility of the parties for the uses to which elective office is put. The parties pursue political power through their candidates for office, but when they win, they hesitate. Are they or are they not to govern — and can they govern even if they choose to? This inability of the parties to account for the power held in their name results, furthermore, in a continuing tension and an ambiguous relationship between the regular party organization and the party in the legislature. It is hard, in fact, to find even one democratic party that has satisfactorily solved the dilemmas of the conflict between national party and legislative party. It is just as difficult to find an electorate that has a consistent set of expectations about the relationship of the national and legislative parties.

THE QUEST FOR PARTY RESPONSIBILITY

In their choice of a phrase to describe the party role they favor, the proponents of party responsibility have almost foreclosed a good share of the argument with a semantic flourish. Clearly no one wants to defend the "irresponsible" party. But the high-sounding euphony of "party responsibility" actually glosses over four distinct components of the concept: the party program, the pledged candidates, the mandate election, and the legislative discipline. The responsible party begins by formulating a coherent and lucid party program or platform well in advance of the election or, ideally, before the nominations. It must, second, control the nomination of candidates sufficiently to ensure the selection of candidates who recognize and express their loyalty to the party program. Third, at the election — in which parties and candidates would presumably contest chiefly on the issues they support — the voters will choose between them, at least to some extent, on these programmatic distinctions. The election offers an occasion for an electoral majority to mandate its representatives to pursue a set of preferred policies. Finally, the winning candidates move to enact their program into public policy, aided, if necessary, by the discipline of a watchful political party.

The rationale for this model of party responsibility rests chiefly on a dissatisfaction with present relationships within the democracies between individual voters and distant, remote policy makers. The parties in the mass, popular democracies, so the argument goes, must organize meaningful policy alternatives for the voters. They alone can organize both majorities of voters and majorities of policy makers and then unite the two majorities in the pursuit of unified, explicit policy goals. The alternative to party responsibility, obviously, can be seen in the present American party system. It is a system of compromising, moderate parties with no identifiable and separable issue commitments. The parties present candidates for office largely on non-issue grounds and eventually leave them to work out pragmatic, moderate policies should they win office.

Advocacy of party responsibility represents, at the level of the entire political system, a rebellion against inactive, deadlocked, or minimal government and against a contentment with the status quo in public policy. It would eliminate undisciplined legislators moving out of alliance with their fellow partisans and into coalitions with the other party, and it rejects what appears to be a piecemeal, temporizing approach to public problems. The advocates see the strong, centralized, ideological political party as the single agent that can bind the disparate elements of the political system together for unified programs of action and for imaginative, sweeping assaults on contemporary American problems.

The desirability of the "more responsible" political parties, then, hinges on the desirability of the whole mélange of sub-goals on which the call for responsibility rests. The "responsibilitarians" want action and change; they favor a full-range, programmatic attack on the needs and demands of society. They prefer positive, vigorous, responsive government as the most efficacious solver of public problems. They are, furthermore, prepared to see the end of legislative independence and to force legislative parties to take their policy cues from the party and the political executive. They feel that the free-wheeling American legislature, working out compromises and *modi vivendi* among the many interests in American society, lacks both focus and responsibility. In its unbridled independence and discretion lies the nub of the failure of party stewardship. And since the most likely curb on this legislative independence will come in the American system from the President and governors, the sponsors of the responsible party support vigorous executive action. In short, the sub-goals of the school of responsible parties are these: ideological parties, a questioning of the status quo, executive power, centralization within the American federalism, and the encouragement of strong and positive governmental authority.

Opposition to party responsibility, whether from academic circles or political practitioners, challenges the desirability of such reforms. But the main burden of their counter-criticism has been on the grounds, not of undesirability, but on those of realism, practicability, and possibility. It just can't be done within the limits of the American party and political systems, they say. The ability of the party to shape those differing platforms and programs presumes an ideological and unidimensional politics in which the parties divide a heterogeneous society along the lines of a single issue or set of issues. Indeed, the proponents of responsibility assume that the American society would generate clear-cut, political differences and that these would be apparent to the American electorate, were they not muffled and clouded by the major parties. The assumption is, clearly, that these sharp differences and issues do exist now and need only a party system that will articulate them.

Furthermore, one may wonder whether or not mandate elections can be cultivated even in a contemporary, popular democracy. Rarely do elections have clear meanings beyond the simple facts of who won and lost. To argue that large numbers of voters will see, or can be made to see, the election as a referendum on great policy statements is to ignore all the sober assessments of American voting behavior. Voters may choose candidates out of some identification with ideological or issue positions, but they also vote for a welter of reasons that have nothing to do with issues: traditional party loyalties, the personalities of the candidates, or local group norms or pressures on them. Elections in modern democracies are adapted reasonably well to the selection and recruitment of officeholders, but they are poorly suited as periodic referenda on momentous ideological alternatives. Mandate elections would demand that voters give the highest priority to ideological concerns, that they all select out and react to the same issues on which the election was being contested, and that, finally, someone judge and ascertain the particular issues that had been decided.

If neither the parties nor the election meet the assumptions of responsibility, is it a completely unattainable utopia? What, indeed, of Great Britain, for it is the British example of cohesive parliamentary parties supporting or opposing Cabinet proposals that so many proponents of party responsibility have in mind as their ideal. What one finds in Great Britain, though, is a modified or partial responsibility. The parties do organize cohesive majorities in Commons, and the majority party does furnish the votes to enact the policy its leadership in the Cabinet proposes. The majority party in Commons achieves a high order of discipline and cohesion on major legislative issues, and it does accept responsibility for presenting an extensive program of policy proposals. But those proposals come more from the Cabinet than from the party manifesto or a majority judgment at a general election. The parliamentary parties of both British major parties have, furthermore, stoutly resisted policy dictation by the national organs of their parties. Missing from the model of party responsibility, then, are the elements of sharply divided ideological parties (although they have certainly achieved a greater programmatic identity than the American parties have) and the mandate election.

As a form of responsibility the British version is not markedly different from that achieved in a number of American states in which a cohesive majority enacts a substantial measure of the governor's program, should he be of the same party. To a certain extent we have achieved short periods of a similar variety of responsibility at the national level in crises such as that of the Great Depression that Franklin Roosevelt faced in the One Hundred Days of 1933 and throughout most of the 1930's. The pressure of weighty and threatening events and the overwhelming popular demand for governmental action stamped themselves on the major parties and their candidates. As a result, the parties came very close to meeting the assorted assumptions of responsibility for the short period of the 1930's. The parties acquired a programmatic identification for many Americans, and so did their candidates. The election of 1936 probably came as close to a general mandate election as the United States has seen. The combination of events produced an ideological attention, an electorate divided essentially on a single set of social and economic reform issues, and a quasi-mandate election — the very conditions necessary for a full-blown party responsibility. But the Roosevelt successes before the 1936 election and some similar program victories of American governors are more typical. These approximations of the model of the responsible party might be called a form of indirect responsibility in which the cohesive governing party accepts the policy program of its executive leadership, provides disciplined legislative support for it, and then accepts an ex post facto responsibility for it to the electorate.

These debates over the responsible party and the subsidiary

issues of the role of the party in the processes of democratic government reduce themselves ultimately to a series of questions
about one's concept of representative democracy itself. The argument in favor of responsibility assumes that support for programs
of government action can best be mobilized in the electorate as
a whole. By stating clearly drawn positions, the parties and their
candidates come into office with popular mandates for action.
The election becomes an instrument of policy making as well as
a recruiter of public personnel. The view of representation implicit in the concept of the responsible party sees the representative as a party-pledged agent rather than the freely deliberating,
independent, Burkean legislator. The majorities necessary for the
enactment of policy are to be organized in the process of contesting elections rather than later in the lobbies of a legislature or the
offices of an executive or administrative agency. Above all, the
concept of responsibility sees the political party as the only satis-
factory representational agency in a popular democracy. It alone
can capture, organize, and transmit the whole range of interests
and aspirations within a large and plural society.

The exploration of a theory and philosophy of democracy is,
happily, well beyond the scope of this essay. The plea for party
responsibility, however, appears to rest on a naive theory of democracy that one would have difficulty squaring with the complex reality of the world's democracies. To say that it expects too
much of the political parties is to miss the point. It really expects
too much knowledge, too much attention, too much involvement
of the American electorate. It underestimates the impact on political parties and the political system of the conflicting, complex,
disorderly demands of a plural society. Consequently, it sorely
underestimates the difficulty and subtleties of the processes by
which consensus and political support emerge in a democracy.
Finally, it tends to picture democratic consent and consensus as
moving mainly in one direction — from the individual and small,
primary groups, up through the parties and great aggregates of
voters, and finally to public officials in legislatures and executives.
Consent moves from bottom to top on a democratic conveyor
belt. Little room seems to remain for the possibility that policy

makers will frame policy alternatives and build consent for them, or that they will make policy in an opinion vacuum.

PARTY IN THE AMERICAN COURTS AND EXECUTIVES

The pursuit of democracy begins even in its most rudimentary form with the election box. The control of governmental power, according to democratic tenets, can most effectively be ensured by making its wielders come periodically before an electorate. Worship of the ballot box has reached new heights in the United States. Not even the judiciary has escaped the electoral mystique. Throughout the United States judges are recruited, appointed, and elected under party auspices. One must, therefore, ask whether or not the parties have sought to use and mobilize their partisan power within the judiciary.

Within the federal judiciary all judges are appointed to the bench by the President with the advice and consent of the Senate. In this century the Presidents have appointed between 80 and 95 per cent of the judges they named from the ranks of their own parties. Had the Republicans not been forced to appoint Democrats to Southern judgeships, the cumulative percentage would be significantly higher. The federal judgeships constitute a body of useful, high-level patronage for the reward of lawyers active in politics. Just to whose patronage the judgeships belong is not an easy matter to settle. Some of the recipients have been active in general party leadership circles; others have come, thanks to "senatorial courtesy," from the personal entourage of senators or from local party supporters of the President himself. Despite the partisan experience and qualifications of the federal judges, no one has suggested that the parties have even attempted to mobilize their former activists on the bench. Nor is there any evidence that the judges themselves break into party blocs on any of the collegial courts. Once the federal bench has served its patronage function, the party has done with it.

In some of the states the parties use the judiciary for the same patronage purposes as the federal judiciary. But in other states the judge-party relationship endures beyond appointment. Especially in those courts in which judges are elected for short terms, some studies have noted the tendency for judges of a state supreme court to divide repeatedly along old party lines in constitutional and statutory interpretation. Although the parties attempt no external party discipline — usually — the justices may have assimilated the values and interests the party represents. Their party service and ties, in other words, indicate and even reinforce a personal system of values, which they take as intellectual baggage with them to the court. Beyond those ties, the judge chosen after years of devoted service to the party may carry to the bench a loyalty to that party, its leadership, and its immediate interests as a party. The impression, extremely difficult to document, does exist among serious observers of some state courts that judges tend to be solicitous of the party's interests in cases directly affecting them — cases applying state party, election, or corrupt practices acts, or those dealing with contested elections and legislative apportionment.

With the American executive, President or governor, the political party has a much more explicit and reciprocal relationship. Defined only sketchily in constitutions and the product of a particular fear of personal power, the American political executive has found in the leadership of a political party the main source of his expanding extra-constitutional powers. For him the political party is both a means for organizing popular support and an instrument with which to prod recalcitrant legislators.

The President finds himself naturally drawn to leadership of his national party by the very nature of the separation of powers, which throws him into calculated conflict with the legislative party. The national party nominated and elected him, and it looks on his office and its perquisites as the chief rewards of national party power. The national party and the President both reflect the popular, mass, nationalizing politics of the Presidential nominating convention and campaign, rather than the political localism of the Congressional party. They represent a constituency defined by the Electoral College and oriented to the cities and large, populous states. The Congressional party springs from individual senatorial and house districts, most of which magnify the political power of rural and small-town groups. The President in effect runs the national party through his personal choice for the national party chairmanship. Perhaps nothing establishes the merging of the Presidency with the national party more clearly than the fact that for the party that loses the Presidential election and has no Presidential leadership, the national party literally disintegrates until the next nominating convention.

Presidential and gubernatorial ties to the national and state parties grow out of the imperatives of the American separation of powers. They contrast, understandably, with the party–executive relationship of the parliamentary political systems. The prime minister and his fellow cabinet members come to their positions because they are the parliamentary leadership of a national party. They owe their offices to their legislative party and depend on its continuing support for the enactment of cabinet policies. Although they may have differences with the national party organs and councils, they engage them as members of the legislative party, not of an executive or cabinet wing of the party. In the parliamentary-cabinet systems, in other words, parliamentary party discipline joins cabinet and parliament together into a single policy-making system. Parliamentary systems produce divisions between policy makers and a national party speaking for local party units, a national party bureaucracy and apparatus, and party members and adherents. The division within the American system tends much more to pit the partisans in one branch of government against another, with each attempting to draw on vague loyalties to party and on the strength of an almost nonexistent national party.

Presidential domination or leadership of the national political party, in fact, usually means only that the President uses the party as a mobilizer of support for his legislative program and his own re-election. Rarely does he use his leadership to build or reshape the party organization itself. President Eisenhower did initially plan to use his Presidential prestige to liberalize his political party toward a "progressive conservatism" or a "new Republicanism." He eventually lost interest in the reform, however, as he himself was increasingly drawn to the conservatism he had earlier sought to alter. Generally, even as powerful a President as Franklin Roosevelt and the stronger American governors have preferred to use their limited supply of patronage and political leverage for legislative rather than organizational purposes. It is, therefore, only in a symbolic sense that the political executive leads the party. He attaches himself and his prestige to it, drawing from it the identifications and loyalties its members and adherents have toward it. To it he contributes whatever popularity and successes he may have and whatever patronage he may see fit to divert to it. Only rarely does he concern himself with the party as an enduring political organization. The party remains for him the most useful personal following and instrument of executive power and leadership.

The executives, mayors through the American President, also control the relationship between the party and the administration. At one time the administrative services were the great incentive banks of American politics. They yielded not only patronage jobs, but most of the other immediate rewards of politics as well — the awarding of contracts, the special treatment and special services for the party faithful, the tolerance of illicit activity, the differential enforcement of legal standards. In many state and local governments the old uses have been little disturbed. In others, the United States government for instance, only the top administrative positions remain for executive appointment. And they must be used not only as political rewards, but also to ally top administrators with the President and his program. In this sense, the political party approaches a new, administration-centered form of party responsibility. Party provides the administrative discipline behind a Presidential program on which the Presidential party must stand or fall in future elections.

PARTY IN THE AMERICAN LEGISLATURES

Although the American parties have unmistakable ties to the courts and executive branches, their presence in American legislatures is far more obvious. The arguments in favor of more responsible parties center on the legislative party as if their proponents accepted the popular myth that only legislative branches make public policy. It is true, though, that of the three branches only the legislature has its own party sub-organizations within the main party apparatus. The place of the legislative party in the precinct-to-national-committee hierarchy of the major

American parties, however, remains one of the chief unsolved organizational quandaries of the parties. Few parties in any of the democracies have integrated the legislative party into the lines of authority of the regular party structure. Usually it stands apart from the national party, a bit like an independent and wealthy uncle who fears the pleas and supplications of an improvident family. Most legislative parties, certainly including the American, enjoy their own reward system and an independent base of political power. They can ignore the national party, and are suspicious of its friendly overtures.

All legislative parties are anomalies in their party systems. They share the party's label, its traditions, and at least nominally, its leadership and its fortunes. And yet as a league of officeholders the legislative party seeks only re-election and looks with disfavor on party activities beyond the purely electoral. It is a local party, the product of a conglomeration of local constituencies, and it distrusts attempts to define national party policies and goals. Democratic Congressional leaders in the mid-1950's balked at attempts to set up a Democratic Advisory Council to speak in policy matters for the national Democratic party. Republicans in Congress developed no greater enthusiasm for a national Republican Committee on Program and Progress (the Percy committee), a group appointed under President Eisenhower's aegis to draft a statement of purpose for national Republicans.

Success in the legislative party follows a route of its own. It begins and continues with election and re-election, but in addition success comes with skill in legislating and in admittance to the inner circles of the legislature. The leader of the legislative party has the arts of the campaigner and the legislator, but he usually has little experience in the management of the party organization. Furthermore, the legislative party has its own self-contained system of rewards that it alone controls — the positions of legislative leadership, the desirable committee assignments, the success of one's bills and resolutions, the acceptance of one's colleagues. In political goals, experience, and values the legislative party often has little in common with the oligarchs and bureaucrats of the national party or state parties. Its main loyalties are to the legislative party, the group life, and the traditions of the legislature.

It expects that the holders of the positions of legislative leadership it confers will recognize the overriding norms of the legislature rather than those of a national party.

In fact, even though the political party in the American legislature bestows power in the name of the party, it rarely acts as a political party. In Congress and most state legislatures the legislative party has little disciplinary power over the rank and file of the party membership, and party conferences and caucuses rarely attempt to bind their members. What discipline the legislative party is able to generate is discipline in its own interests, those of the legislative leadership, or those of a powerful executive of its party. As a party it is diffused and splintered within itself by the dispersal of the power of the legislative chamber. As Ranney and Kendall write:

> . . . there is no locus of concentrated power in either house of Congress that might enable a party to translate its program into legislation via steam-roller or push-button tactics. The power of a congressional majority is highly fragmented, so that bits and pieces of it are lodged in floorleaders, standing committees, committee chairmen, presiding officers, and rules committees, among whom there may be countless differences of opinion and emphasis. . . .

The legislative party, in other words, acts only infrequently out of loyalty to the national party or even in pursuit of goals and interests of the party as a party, rather than of the party as a group of individual legislators.

Open warfare between the legislative party and the national party has racked many of the parties of Europe. The mass-membership, ideological parties of the left have attempted the fullest domination of the parliamentary party. The Socialist party of postwar France, for example, imposes penalties that include censure, suspension, and even expulsion of legislators ignoring party discipline. Even suspension removes the member as a candidate for re-election and deprives him of his positions on parliamentary committees. Such electoral sanctions, one might add, were facilitated by the party's control of the listing of candidates for election in a proportional-representation system. But the freedom of the legislative party mounts in the non-ideological, cadre parties of the right and center. Legislative parties find it easier to make their peace with parties which share their electoral preoccupation and which have no active clienteles or explicit program vying with the legislators for the right to commit the party on policy decisions.

Ultimately the legislative party maintains its freedom and power only at the sufferance of an ineffectual national party. When the national party is at best a coalition of local electoral parties, without any independent leadership or bureaucracy, it can hardly master the legislative party. In the American system the feeble, elusive national party — even when allied with the popular leadership, the administrative patronage, and the constitutional powers of the Presidency — offers no match for the entrenched and continuing power of the legislative party. And when it has no Presidential power with which to ally, its position deteriorates to complete ineffectuality. During the Eisenhower years the Democratic majority leader in the Senate, Lyndon B. Johnson, assumed the de facto leadership of the party without serious challenge. And during the first Kennedy term Representative Halleck and Senator Dirksen, the Republican Congressional leadership, exercised a condominium over the national Republican image and personality. When former President Eisenhower attempted in the summer of 1962 to set up an All-Republican Conference as a spokesman for the evanescent national party, the Congressional party objected. Senator Goldwater, chairman of the Senate Republican Campaign Committee, rejected it out of hand, and press reports indicated that the Dirksen-Halleck duo was greatly restrained in its enthusiasm.

Conflict between the Congressional and Presidential representatives of the party stems primarily from the conflict and competition of the American separation of powers. It is exaggerated, furthermore, by the differences in the constituencies and electorates that choose each of them. It is not merely that one represents a constituency of the parts and the other a constituency of the whole. The Congressional constituencies collectively over-represent rural and small-town America. The Presidential constituency, defined by the Electoral College, over-represents the large urban states whose large blocks of electoral votes figure so prominently in the strategies of most Presidential candidates. Presidential parties, therefore, tend to represent the "liberalism" of lower socio-economic groups and urban minorities. Furthermore, the Congressional party represents, collectively, the one-party areas in which they are secure and isolated from many political currents and issues. The President, on the other hand, represents the competitive national constituency and the resultant need to make the broadest, most comprehensive political appeal. Finally, the overlap of leadership between legislative and Presidential-national party that characterizes many parliamentary parties does not mark the American parties. Even when the national parties have chosen legislators as national committee chairmen, they have chosen men such as Senator Thruston Morton and Representative William Miller, both Republicans, who have not been legislative leaders.

Any device or reform that would bring the Presidential and Congressional parties closer together has always attracted support purely on the grounds of minimizing the divisions of the separation of powers. Behind most of the proposals for party responsibility is a preference for Presidential party control of an unruly and independent Congressional party in the name of a national consensus within the party. Yet, the critics overlook even the few ties that bind these two groups of partisans together. Presidential patronage and appointments come to Congressional parties only with the success of the Presidential party. Furthermore, the Congressional party has to stand or fall on the record the President does or does not make in office. The President and Presidential leadership tend increasingly to dominate the popular image of the party. The Congressional wing of the party, though it is protected in its localities by personal followings and one-party politics, cannot completely escape the popular identification of the President with the party. Finally, the members of the Congressional party recognize the power of the Presidential coattails in bringing some of their fellow partisans into Congress. The Southern Democrats in Congress, for instance, know that their committee chairmanships depend on achieving majority status in the House and Senate. Many also see the importance of the Presidential candidate to the election and re-election of many fellow

Democrats who come from competitive districts. In fact, the Southern contingent of the Democratic legislative party has generally opposed their state parties' moves to bolt the national party in disappointment over national candidates and platforms.

PARTY RESPONSIBILITY IN THE UNITED STATES

The whole concept of party responsibility presumes the existence of legislative majorities that will enact party policy. In the British parliamentary system cohesion in the House of Commons reflects both the ability of the party to discipline its mavericks, even by denying them renomination in extreme cases, and the disciplining pressures of the need to support and oppose a cabinet. The American separation of powers, however, does not require the legislature or a legislative majority to bear responsibility to a national electorate or to support an executive program. It does not, indeed, grant the fullness of power for which a party might be held responsible. The philosophy of the separation of powers rests on the control of governmental power through a system of internal checks, limits, and countervailing power. The British system, on the other hand, grants unchecked reservoirs of power to party majorities on the assumptions of control and responsibility to an external electorate and popular judgment. External responsibility through a political party is, therefore, consistent with basic British constitutional philosophy, but the American constitutional arrangements rely on internal limitations.

Party responsibility in its fullest form would demand an electorate attuned to policy issues, parties capable of enunciating them, and elections at which candidates were chosen because of their programmatic commitments. Those conditions seem unlikely to prevail in any two-party system with the massive, majority parties it breeds. And, ironically, the idea of a responsible party relates only to those two-party systems in which legislative majorities are possible. The dilemma is clear. Those parties which can meet the party and electoral canons of responsibility cannot meet the need for cohesive legislative majorities, and those, such as the American, which can possibly provide the cohesive majorities, cannot relate them to an ideological party or electorate.

Legislative cohesion or discipline alone is not equivalent to the classic party responsibility, however. Discipline is a necessary but not a sufficient condition of responsibility. The question becomes, therefore, what sort of responsibility the party fashions out of legislative cohesion.

Cohesion in the American legislatures varies greatly within the federal system. In some of the competitive, two-party states — such as Connecticut, New York, and Pennsylvania — studies have indicated high degrees of party cohesion on non-unanimous votes. The United States Congress has approached their levels of cohesion at various times over the past generation or so. Such discipline, unachieved by the majority of state legislatures, reflects four main pressures for cohesion on the legislature. There are, first of all, the instruments of executive pressure: the patronage, his leadership of the party, the strength of his office. Then, the strength and persuasion of the legislative leadership and caucus produce discipline in the legislative party. Third, one might cite the party orientation of the legislator himself. His years of membership or work in the party may have created loyalties and identifications with the party, especially if it has chosen him from its ranks to run for office. He may also represent and accept the interests of dominant groups within the party; in fact, the chances are good that he is a member of them. The occupational, ethnic, and religious backgrounds of Democrats and Republicans differ greatly in the legislatures of most competitive states. Finally, the similar constituencies of members of the same legislative party put them under a similar set of constituency pressures and direct them into a cohesive legislative group. The strength or weakness of these four pressures explains why the legislative parties of one state exhibit a greater degree of cohesion than those of another.

Usually this legislative cohesion or discipline supports political programs, not of the party organization outside of government and in the electorate, but of either the executive or the legislative leadership. Therefore, the closest the American parties come and are likely to come to the model of the responsible party, except under the stress of conditions approaching a national emergency, is this:

1. Legislative parties cohere because of legislative leadership and norms, executive pressure, loyalty to the party and its dominant interests, and the pressure of constituencies with similar interests.

2. Those cohesive legislative parties support either executive programs or *ad hoc* proposals of the legislative leadership, which at best may reflect the dominant interests (and their typical constituencies), the "silent ideology," within the party coalition.

3. That program becomes a part of the general impressions the electorate has of the party and its leadership. In some indirect, almost haphazard way, it filters into their awareness and perception of the party and colors their reactions to the party and its candidates in future elections.

So, only fitfully and tentatively do the parties govern. The unified, almost monolithic direction of the responsible political party is beyond them. National and state parties in the United States cannot recast the political dialogue into programmatic or ideological terms, and they cannot relate the cohesion of the legislative party to the hierarchy of the party organization or to its voters and adherents.

The entire debate over the desirability and/or possibility of more responsible political parties brings one, ultimately, to the basic questions of the role of the political party in a democratic political system. The school of party responsibility would like the American parties to extend themselves beyond their electoral preoccupations to state programs and discipline the officeholders they have elected. In effect, party responsibility calls for an expansion of the role of the political party beyond its present predominantly electoral function. At the same time, it seeks the growth of the party's power so that it can assert a monopoly over the three main political functions. Within a political system dominated by the responsible party there is no room for alternative agencies, such as interest groups and informal political elites, to organize consent, support policy alternatives, and direct the work of legislatures. The plea for party responsibility asks, in other words, for party control of the major points of access in the political process and for party monopoly of the representative processes that join individual citizens and the decision makers of government.

Any such reform of the American parties confronts, inevitably, the question of whether or not the parties are infinitely malleable institutions whose partisans determine their functions. What the party is and what it does are not so completely at its own pleasure. Its tasks are determined by the imperatives of the political system as a whole and by the political culture of the society. With these issues — and they are those of a general theory of the political party — the following two chapters are concerned.

8

The party
and its environment

Most of the constitutions of the 19th-century democracies, and earlier ones such as the American, make little or no mention of political parties. Their framers either did not foresee the rise of the political party to the role it presently occupies, or else they considered the party an extra-constitutional excrescence not to be dignified by mention in the constitutional document. In either case the political party appeared as an unplanned adjunct to the formal political institutions and processes. It was never given the full legal or constitutional status its functions merited, nor was it conceded to play an important role in the formal political system.

Scholars of this century have made a parallel failure to integrate an understanding of the party and the party system into a general description and theory of the political system. Much of the study of political parties has abstracted them from other political institutions and processes and studied them *in vacuo*. We have long tended to view the party as an infinitely changeable and adaptable institution that men can develop into any political instrument they wish, regardless of the limits and bounds that the party's political environment sets for it. At this late date these omissions and failings seem far less excusable than the failure of the American founding fathers to foresee the development and growing importance of parties. The result, in any event, has been the absence of a full-scale theory of parties. That theory must begin with some understanding of the relationships between the party and its political environment: the context in which the party operates, to which it responds, and by which it is shaped. Since the party is essentially an organizational and transmitting agent that operates within the interstices and institutions of the formal political structure, what it is will be greatly determined by the nature of the political interests it organizes and the political system for which it organizes.

The environment in which the party operates and to which it responds includes not only the formal structures of government, but also a maze of statutory regulations and provisions that control and affect the interests of the parties as organizations. It also includes the political values and political cultures that define general opinions of what a party should be, what it should do, and the rules of taste and propriety that govern the ways in which it can act. Storks do not bring political parties. Both in structure and in function they are no more independent of a political culture and the context of the political system than are a state legislature, a city manager, or the United States Supreme Court. With that realization one takes the first step toward the development of a theory of political parties.

PARTIES AND THE POLITICAL REGIME

In this essay we have been examining only the parties of the democracies, with especial emphasis on the parties and the party system of the American democracy. That implicit limit recognizes both the impact of a democratic system on the parties and the characteristics that divide them from the parties of the non-democratic regimes. The democratic parties are deeply involved in the representation of political interests, the recruitment of popular leadership, the free competition of political preferences, and the mobilization of majorities — functions that touch the very heart of the democratic processes. The parties of the non-democratic states function more directly in the management of opinion, the selection of political activists, and the uses of formal, governmental power in the name of an established political elite.

But there are democracies and democracies. The nature of the democratic traditions and their postulates create different environments for the parties. Universal adult suffrage for a literate population usually effectively and naturally creates a set of expectations about participation and democracy within the political party that the narrowly based, cadre party has a harder time meeting than does the mass, popular party. The American parties have, however, been one of the few exceptions to that rule, possibly because of the generally low esteem in which they have been held. But many of the remaining American democratic traditions have been stamped on the American parties. The American constitution and democratic practice have from the very beginning had profoundly anti-majoritarian aspects that grew out of a fear of unlimited majoritarian tyranny and a concern for the rights and interests of minorities. Whether that anti-majoritarianism was expressed in formal institutions such as the separation of powers and the Electoral College or in pervasive attitudes about democracy, it has forced the American parties to swim constantly upstream in their attempts to build cohesive majorities. Theirs has been the difficult task of mobilizing majority power in a political system that, despite its democratic faith, is suspicious of majority power. The American democracy places less faith in the control of government by aroused and informed popular majorities than does, say, the British. Its reliance on the almost mechanistic balancing and reciprocating pulls and tugs of antagonistic powers and institutions as limits to the uses of power leaves little room for the political party that would relate policy decisions and issues back to watchful majorities in the electorate.

Furthermore, since the essence of representative democracy concerns the ephemeral and fragile relationship between the full electorate and a selected group of policy makers, the prevailing approaches to representation cannot fail to have their impact on the parties. The tendency of many Americans to accept a neo-Burkean theory of representation that recognizes the desirability of the free, rational, unfettered representative acting in the best interests of the locality or the entire polity seems hardly compatible with party discipline of candidates, much less with any more grandiose theories of responsible political parties. Also, a democratic ideology that has no real ideology, that has never demanded an awareness of public issues or alternatives, and that even makes a virtue out of low levels of public involvement, inevitably leaves political decisions to the informed and interested few. The role and responsibility of the electorate lies chiefly in giving or withholding, ex post facto, its approval after sampling the results. Under such democratic conditions, the role of the American parties as defined by the American democracy appears to be little more than that of facilitating the contesting of elections as a way of recruiting representatives and of measuring their stewardship.

Much of the explanatory material of this book so far has elaborated on the ways in which the parliamentary-cabinet systems affect the political parties in ways quite different from the American Presidential system. Cabinet government concentrates party leadership and merges it with the party's elected officials. The result is a tightening of party discipline within the legislative party and a greater policy-making role for the party as a whole. The American Presidential system introduces and institutionalizes executive leadership as party leadership, sets the legislative party apart from the rest of the party apparatus, and generally fragments the party within the political system. The separation of powers militates against the development of responsible parties by discouraging and preventing the mobilization of a single, all-embracing majority within the American political system. It also enhances the power of dominant personalities in American politics by allying executive leadership with the party apparatus and image.

Similarly, the geographical or areal distribution of governmental authority demands a party structure that parallels its placement of public offices and electoral constituencies. Not only must the American party structure match, constituency for constituency, the dispersed authority of a federal system, but also the mere existence of separate, local governments offers tremendous impetus to and rewards for political localism. The local political units have elective offices, patronage, and local loyalties and traditions that nourish the local party. The American federalism, no exception to the general impact of federalism, has produced a party system of almost total decentralization in which local party organizations have become almost completely independent of the help and authority of central, national party organs. The decentralizing drive of federalism, one should add, does not result only from the decentralization of government. It is additionally a product of the sheer size of the partisan job that results from the many elections to many short terms for many public officials in many political subdivisions over a country with the expanse and population of the United States. Finally, the American federalism has encouraged the development of areas of one-party politics in the United States, with all of the attendant effects that one-partyism brings to the parties.

This part of the parties' environment that we call the political regime extends beyond the institutions of government to the social and economic structures and activity within the society. They define the nature of the electorate with which the party works, and they provide the materials of political controversy and issues with which the parties cope. The age and educational composition of an electorate, its income and employment levels, and its religious and ethnic composition determine the general interests, groups, and loyalties of the electorate for which the parties compete. To be more specific, when the new industrial working classes rose in the present century, the parties either had to bid successfully for their support or reconcile themselves to their expression in new parties and new political movements. As it happened in Europe, the existing liberal parties failed to accommodate the new industrial proletariat, leaving them to form new labor, socialist, and eventually communist parties. And as old classes decline in importance, parties based on them either adapt or decline; hence the passage of the European liberal parties, which were built on an early commercial and mercantile class: the English Liberals, the German Center party, and the French Radical-Socialists (who were, of course, neither radical nor socialist).

Within the American political system the general social mobility in the American society and the absence of a feudal tradition support a fluid and mobile electorate in which no individual, group, or class has been irrevocably associated with any particular party.

From such social materials have emerged the pragmatic, brokerage, pluralistic politics of the American parties. The American social system has not been conducive to sharp and firm party divisions along lines of either class or ideology. More specific social events and changes also have influenced the American parties. The Great Depression of the 1930's in the United States reshaped the issues of American politics and redrafted the American electorate into a party division along clearer socio-economic class and interest lines. Great shocks such as this to the basic social institutions and the social equilibrium bring shifts and dislocations of enduring strength in parties and politics. Even slower, more subtle social changes do. Certainly the gradual assimilation of Roman Catholic religious-ethnic groups into American society on an equal footing with older American elites lies behind the nomination and the election of John F. Kennedy to the Presidency when it was widely conceded less than a generation before that no Catholic could be elected President.

There is, indeed, little or nothing about the political parties that cannot be affected by these changes in the more general social institutions and culture. Their organization reflects the institutions of government, the value of their incentives may depend on social prejudice or unemployment rates, and they carry out their electing function in the context of issues and expectations set by broader social forces. Even the social and political assets of a would-be Presidential candidate — those characteristics the parties somewhat misleadingly refer to as his "availability" — reflect basic social values and structures. Whether or not the parties dare nominate a divorced man or a Roman Catholic depends entirely on them.

THE REGULATION OF PARTY AND POLITICS

It is probable that no other democracy imposes a heavier yoke of regulation and hedging-about on its political parties than does the United States. The statutes of some of the American states even go to the trouble of fixing the time and places of the meetings of various party units. And this overt regulation is only a part of the statutory limitations the parties feel. They are subject also to a vast amount of "unintentional" regulation in that they are affected by policy enacted for other reasons that have incidental, but often potent, consequences for the parties. Some states, for reasons that have nothing to do with the affairs and health of the parties, may extend the absentee ballot to students living away from home while attending college. Yet, the change alters the scope and nature of the electorate, and thus affects the parties intimately.

The American regulation of the nature and operations of the parties stands almost alone among attempts in the democracies to regulate the parties. Each of the 50 states is free to define a political party, to outline its organization, define who will choose party leaders and in what manner they will choose, and set limits to the financing of party operations. Few states have failed to take up the challenge. Their varied, shifting, often harassing regulations are to the American parties what state-fixed weight limit, load distribution, and safety requirements are to the interstate trucking industry. The states have, too, used their power of regulation to outlaw political parties and to deny them access to the ballot in the state, a power most recently invoked to the disadvantage of the American Communist party. Finally, the states have controlled the parties' nomination of candidates for public office through their adoption of the direct primary. Certainly no more need be said of it here.

This full range of regulation has forced and encouraged the American parties into a series of adaptations, modifications, and ruses by which they co-exist with their regulators. In general they have shown an ability to adapt to new environments that seems almost organic or biological in its uncanniness. Within the party whose formal convention must meet too late to endorse candidates for the primary, an informal, pre-primary meeting may develop and may eventually be institutionalized. Party response to state financial regulations has been a dictionary of evasions and avoidances: "dummy" contributors who lend their names to real contributors seeking anonymity, voluntary political committees that do not have to report their finances, fragmented giving, and simple refusal to make full and specific reports. In a number of other states some of the party committees established by law simply do not exist in any active form; parties may be regulated, but they cannot be created by legislative fiat. More generally, this regulation of the American parties produces discontinuous, decentralized, and non-adaptive party organization that has trouble meeting demands for new mass-membership, middle-class politics. The old-style politics of the turn of the century has been embedded and preserved in inflexible and unchanging statutes. They account in great measure for the chaotic, defensive, often secretive style and behavior of the American parties. If they often seem furtive, they have good reason to be.

Statutory regulation of the party includes a second general type of environmental control: the defining of the electorate and the franchise. Electorates only expand in democracies; they rarely contract, short of the complete abandonment of democratic forms. The history of the parties in the Western democracies can be written in the continual absorption of new groups into the party electorates as they were released from property qualifications and restrictions based on sex, race, and religion. Even though the American parties are not at present vying to expand the suffrage of Negroes in many parts of the country, they compete for their support once they have been enfranchised. Until the adult suffrage in a political system is full and universal, it will be an inaccurate and distorted sample of the community or society. One party or the other will profit by the distortion, and others will lose by it.

The addition of new groups to the electorate, therefore, does not affect all parties equally. It is likely that one or several parties could compete more successfully than others at a given time and in a given political system for the vote of 18-year-olds. Any removal of present limits on the American franchise — those growing out of racial or ethnic prejudice, poll taxes, residence requirements, literacy tests, for example — would add to the electorate lower socio-economic groups that might be expected, in the short run at least, to support the national Democratic party. The question of whether or not to enfranchise Negroes, migrant workers, and non-English-speaking Puerto Ricans is, therefore, highly charged with immediate political consequences. Even the system of registration of voters may have a direct impact on the parties. Those systems which demand periodic re-registration, whatever their advantages may be, tend to disenfranchise poorly educated groups and citizens of low civic interest and involvement. Understandably, also, the American parties prefer registration with party designation not only for its limiting of the primary electorate, but also for the list of partisans it gives the parties to work with.

Laws forbidding political activity of civil servants beyond voting and passive membership in a political party in Great Britain and the United States, though they do not alter the party electorates, do restrict their sources of available manpower and leadership. More than one local party in the United States has seen its leadership corps decimated as the party leaders, one by one, accepted Federal or state office in reward for party activity.

The American parties have also had to pay special attention to those regulations and statutes which touch upon their incentive systems. If the party is chiefly ideological, it faces the dilemmas of success rather than the inroads of public policy. Many of the early independence movements in the developing areas depended heavily on the unifying cry for freedom and independence to hold together disparate and potentially fractious groups and tribes. Once the granting of independence robbed them of their ideological focus, a number of them fell to divisive squabbling; others seized on national economic development as a new ideology. But the American parties have relied on incentives and rewards of a much more tangible sort, and they often find that shifts in policy and statute have disturbed their supply and availability. The American municipality that adopts the "non-fixable" parking and traffic ticket may deprive the party of a much-appreciated gesture of local influence. The expansion of merit systems also has closed off valuable patronage for the parties, just as the expansion of social-welfare programs pre-empts another form of party largesse.

ELECTION LAW: THE RULES OF THE GAME

Because the political parties universally contest elections, no part of their political environment impinges as relentlessly as the electoral system. It distorts the numbers of votes the party collects as it translates that vote total into electoral wins and losses. That power gives it, and its framers, a virtual life-and-death sanction over the political party. For the parties the electoral system operates very much as the mirrors in the carnival fun house, making the thin look fat and the fat thin. At the immediate and practical level, in most of the democracies the question of whether or not a party capable of capturing 10 to 20 per cent of the popular vote will win any seats in a national legislature depends largely on the nature of the electoral system. The sheer magnitude of the impact an electoral system may have on party fortunes can be illustrated by a brief reference to the 1951 elections for the Indian national parliament. The Congress party, because of its national scope, won 73 per cent of the seats with only 45 per cent of the popular vote. The electoral system, in other words, made it into a majority party of enormous legislative power.

Tampering and tinkering with the electoral system — with the way in which the constituencies are drawn, the ratio of offices to constituency, the freedom of access to candidacy, the nature of the ballot itself, the quota of votes needed to elect — involve the parties in wranglings and jockeying for advantage that for sheer partisan intensity are without equal. Few issues so galvanize an American legislative party into cohesive action as do these questions. Ideally, one might hope that laws that can enhance or slash the representative force of a party might be considered with the ethics and demands of a democratic system in mind. Realistically, however, the parties react to these issues according to their own immediate interests, and it is largely those interests that determine how they perceive the philosophical issues.

The one aspect of the electoral system over which the American parties have traditionally contended is that of the boundaries of the electoral constituencies themselves. For majority parties it has meant the power to entrench themselves almost permanently by controlling apportionment and district lines. Until the 1961 decision of the Supreme Court bringing districting within the purview of the Federal judiciary, majority parties in the states could design Congressional and state legislative districts with impunity. They juggled populations so that the strength of one party would be exaggerated through the carving of low-population districts out of its strongholds. The under-representation of many American cities long affected the Democratic party, which flourished in the urban centers. The more recent phenomenon of the under-represented, burgeoning suburban districts has worked to the general disadvantage of the Republicans. Sometimes, of course, the distortion of party strength resulted from constitutional requirements that counties or towns or other civil divisions be represented, regardless of population inequities.

Beyond the drawing of districts unequal in population, the American parties have elevated another mode of electoral distortion, the "gerrymander," to a minor art form. In the gerrymander the controlling party draws district lines in such a way as to use its vote strength most efficiently in electing candidates while it forces the other party into inefficiencies. That result can be accomplished in one of two ways: either by dividing and diluting pockets of the other party's strength to prevent it from winning seats, or (if its strength is too great for dilution) by bunching its strength into a few districts and forcing it to win elections by large and wasteful majorities. We do not suggest that these tactics of electoral advantages are limited to the American parties. The pocket and rotten boroughs did originate in Great Britain. But control of this element of the political environment is an especially cultivated concern of the American parties. The reason may lie in a number of factors — in, for instance, the great variations in the growth of the American population and the unwillingness of American courts to intervene in legislative districting. But probably it stems chiefly from the existence of the American two-party system. The effects of such district changes would be far less clear and far less predictable in a multi-party system. In a two-party system, however, what works to one party's disadvantage will, almost by definition, work to the other's advantage.

By contrast the multi-party systems of Europe have traditionally tinkered and fussed with the electoral counting system. The conventional wisdom of this strategy argues that the single-member district works to the advantage of the larger parties since it rewards only one party and provides no electoral successes even for the consistent second-runner. Proportional representation, to the contrary, encourages the smaller parties since it divides the representatives among the parties according to the percentage of the party vote. Under most apportionment formulas the party pulling 15 per cent of the popular vote in a five-man constituency would win one seat. But electoral arithmetic is not quite so simple in practice. It may be confused by the pattern of the dispersal of the parties' electorates. In a plurality system smaller parties that can concentrate their vote geographically may elect candidates, but they will not if their electorate extends evenly over the nation. Conversely, though proportional representation will generally work to the advantage of smaller parties, it will help the larger parties whose vote strength is heavily concentrated by shielding them from the loss of votes in large and wasteful majorities. In other words, 80 per cent of the vote is no more useful than 51 per cent in a single-member, plurality system, but it is in a district whose representatives are elected proportionally.

The recent experience of the West German Republic indicates the possibility of combining single-member, plurality elections with proportional representation. Seats in the Bundestag are allocated within the Länder; half of the representatives are chosen from single-member districts, the other half by proportional representation from the Land as a whole. However, under the law governing the 1961 elections a party must win a single-member district or 10 per cent of the popular vote in the Land in order to share in the proportional division of the Land-wide seats. The Christian Democrats, as a broadly based national party, profit by the single-member districts; the Social Democrats, with much of their strength concentrated in the cities and industrial areas, prefer the proportional-representation scheme. The minor parties are on the wane and stand to suffer even more from the minimal requirements for proportional sharing that were designed to cut their representation. In fact, only one party other than the two major ones, the Free Democrats, elected any candidates to the Bundestag in 1961. So, electoral systems do shape parties and party systems. But the West German experience also suggests a point usually overlooked: that parties may also shape electoral systems in order to protect their own interests and the party status quo.

These components of the electoral system are the main ones, but they do not by any means exhaust its effects on the parties. Parties may also be concerned with the form of the ballot. In the United States a form of ballot called the party column ballot, which permits voting the straight party ticket with a single "X", pleases the parties for obvious reasons. The office-block ballot, which groups candidates by office sought rather than party affiliation, does not. The parties may also feel the impact of laws that discourage access to the ballot. In Great Britain the requirement that each party candidate post a deposit of £150 ($420), which he will lose unless he wins one-eighth of the total vote in the district, screens out frivolous contenders and even the smaller parties. Its existence forced the Liberal party in 1957 to pick carefully which districts it would contest lest it impoverish itself with optimism. Some American states also legislate against small and non-competitive parties' access to the primary or general election ballot by requiring them to petition for a place on the ballot if they did not win a fixed percentage of the last election vote.

THE POLITICAL CULTURE

Of all the components of the party environment, by far the most elusive is the political culture. It is composed of the attitudes, the norms, the goals that the members of a political system have for it. It governs not only how they as individuals, or collectively, view the political system and their role in it, but also what they expect and what they tolerate in the behavior of individuals and political organizations. It includes a complex of attitudes and expectations about the political parties that are held by the very electorate that the parties mobilize.

About this American political culture, or any other political culture, we really know very little. It is made up of data that are loose, attitudinal, and highly subjective. The individual himself may hardly recognize the attitudes he holds, and he rarely codifies them or talks about them. From individual to individual they range greatly in sophistication and coverage — from an elemental distrust of government to an involved set of responses and attitudes about all aspects of the political system. Political scientists have developed no hypotheses to compare with those in the "economic culture" of R. H. Tawney and Max Weber, which attempt to relate a particular economic system (capitalism) to a particular set of cultural values and a particular ethos (the Protestant ethic).

In the most general way one can, however, point to the widespread American suspicion of and distaste for politics and politicians as the basic element of the American political culture. The average American is very apt to think, as one former politician has put it, "that by the necessities of his profession a soldier must kill and a politician lie." Repeated surveys of American adults indicate in one way or another their disapproval of the vocation of politics. In 1944 only 18 per cent of a national sample of the National Opinion Research Center said they would like to see a son go into politics as a life work; politics as a career ranked well below those of semi-skilled laborers in their esteem.

In fact, so concentrated and dominant does this attitude become in the middle-class haunts of American suburbia that it colors the entire political life of many suburbs. Close to two-thirds of them have legally established non-partisan government. Of the "no-party" politics of American suburbia Robert Wood has written:

> There is, first of all, an outright reaction against partisan activity, a refusal to recognize that there may be persistent cleavages in the electorate, and an ethical disapproval of permanent group collaboration as an appropriate means for settling public disputes. . . . The political animal is tamed; as the suburbanite approaches the ballot box in local elections, he is expected to strive for a consensus with his friends and neighbors, to seek "the right solution" as distinct from favoring one or another faction of his party.

Ultimately, then, the political culture of a community may produce a flight from the parties and partisanship altogether.

Short of a total escape from politics, the American political culture often leads to a cynical political detachment. American "inside-dopesterism," the political style of David Riesman's "other-directed American," appears to be the final distillation of this detached, shoulder-shrugging skepticism about the political system. The "inside dopester" enjoys speculating about the reasons behind reasons and men behind men, but is unwilling to come to grips with the substance of issues and choices. Such a covert rejection of politics and parties, along with the overt flight from politics, springs from an American innocence about politics. Generations of Americans have thought of a governmental ideal in which public decisions were abstracted from the corrupting quest for political power and the pursuit of self-interest. For them politics ought to be the selfless search for higher social goods and interests untainted by social conflict or personal goal-seeking. Theirs has been a repeated search for the Washington myth, the selfless leader above conflict and contention. Such innocent and oversimplified views reject also the elites and the political divisions of labor so necessary in large, complex political systems. They favor a direct person-to-government relationship unbroken by organized, self-seeking intermediaries such as political parties.

Beyond these generalized attitudes toward politics and politicians, the political culture sets norms and goals for the specifics of party organization and operation. It may decree that some of the incentives the party relies on are "outside the pale." Even though one political culture may accept the ethic of patronage, others may reject it for failing to recognize merit, experience, and qualifications in public appointments. The militant to-the-barricades style of the French working-class suburb might also appall the American laboring community, whereas the political ethos of the large industrial American city literally frightens rural and small-town America. American traditions of political localism, to take another example, work sharply against the party legislative discipline so acceptable in Great Britain. The American political vocabulary, in fact, is replete with idioms that suggest a distaste for disciplined party activity — the "party line," the party "hack," party "bossism." Large numbers of Americans doubtless find it perfectly logical that their libraries subsume the subject classification "patronage" under the more general rubric of "corruption in politics."

Even within one political system there may, furthermore, exist a number of special and local political sub-cultures. The extravagant, stentorian political oratory of the American South marks one aspect of its special political culture. Others have noted the political sub-culture of the Irish and of South- and Eastern-European ethnic groups and its acceptance and support of the classic American urban machine.

Differences in political cultures, or among the sub-cultures within one system, beget differences in party style and modes of operation. Party activities vary in the flair, the tone, and the social image they cultivate. These variations are probably related to social class differences. They are tastes and preferences, aspects of

ways of life, that mark class and status lines as do differing preferences for Scotch and beer, Bach and musical comedy, rep ties and
florid sport shirts. For lower-income groups in the Western
democracies, partisan politics has often been an immediate avenue
to gain and betterment. Their mores have, accordingly, accepted
its discipline, its militancy, its aggressiveness, and even its exploita-
tiveness. It represents an entrée to the distant seats of power, a
means for shaking the centers of privilege. These are, of course,
the very aspects of the party and political life that most offend the
middle- and upper-class political groups: the coarse and brash
tone, the exaggerated oratory and political appeals, the juggernaut
solidarity, and the ruthless discipline. Most studies of the American
opinion on parties and politicians have found, indeed, that suspicion of them increases with the educational and income levels of
the respondents. The political culture, in other words, reflects the
same class and regional differences that the general culture does.

THE AMERICAN PARTY AS INTEREST GROUP

The political parties must operate in a political
environment that is as wide and all-encompassing as the entire
political process. One can view that political process, mechanisti-
cally and simply, as a linear series of events. It begins with the
goals, attitudes, and interests of individuals, the goads and incentives that spur them to political activity, and it ends with the
making of public policy in the more formal institutions of government: the legislatures, courts, cabinets, executives, and administrative agencies. Chiefly, the parties organize and mobilize the
political power between these two end points of the political system. And the political materials at both of them — the political
interests and culture of the electorate and the organizations and
procedures of governmental forms — shape the tasks and structures of the political parties. There is, in fact, very little in the
political system that does not put its stamp on the parties.

To control its political environment the party has two chief
alternatives. It may, in the first place, attack the non-institutional
aspects of the environment — the political culture, the interests,
the political proclivities of the citizens — as an educational problem. The party can, in other words, attempt a reconstruction in

political socialization or education. The parties may succeed in societies and political systems, such as those of the developing nations, in which they have few competitors in socialization. It becomes progressively harder, however, as the party shares the function with public education, voluntary organizations, and the literate influence-wielders of the community. What successes the parties enjoy in this task are largely the result of party activities that are directed to young people or that are superficially "non-political." The party-sponsored boy scout troup or youth movement, the social club for senior citizens — these and other activities have as their main political role the creation of values and loyalties that will bind voters to the parties. The successes vary, though. The efforts of European parties to build strong youth groups have had some success, but the comparatively feeble efforts of the American parties to reach the hundreds of thousands of incipient voters in American colleges and universities have not.

The parties' alternative path of action is an attack on that part of the political environment which is institutional and is largely the result of laws and constitutions. It is here the parties become interest groups on their own behalf. As with any other interest groups, they become involved in lobbying bills through legislatures, in seeking changes in administrative interpretation or application of statutes, and in litigating judicial interpretation of law. In doing so they are in the anomalous position of being both more and less than the ordinary interest group. If it is in the majority, the party's access may be far better than that available to the ordinary interest group. But the fact that it is a political party, and hence identified with itself, robs it of the flexibility, the wide and multi-partisan access, the limited area of conflict on which the heady lobbyist and interest group capitalizes. Party lines so harden when a party or the parties become interest groups that sheer numbers usually foretell the result. Generally, only a majority party or an alliance of parties can act.

The materials of this chapter and those before it raise issues of the influences determining party organization and the nature of the party tasks in the political system. They define again the problem of the place of the party in the political process and the politi-

cal environment. Does the political party shape the political contest and the organization of political power, or is it merely the
resultant of a combination of social-cultural and political factors?
These are questions that can be answered only with a theory of the
political party.

9

Toward a theory
of the political party

THE time is hardly ripe in the study of political parties for an announcement of a mature and full-blown theory of parties. Scholarship in this field has not yet even managed a comprehensive descriptive survey of American parties and their activities. The scholarly storehouse, moreover, holds far less on the parties and party systems of the other democracies.

It may not be premature, however, to say that some of the general relationships we have shown within the party and between the party and the socio-political world around it, as well as the analytical categories assigned to those relationships, eventually may be of theoretical value. In this chapter we offer a way of visualizing the parties and their place in the political system — and, more optimistically, a scheme for the description and analysis of political parties and some fragments of a theory of political parties.

BASIC DATA AND RELATIONSHIPS

Throughout the descriptions in this essay of the American political parties and their natural habitat the data on which it has depended have fallen into two main groups: data on the political parties and data concerning the political context or environment in which the parties operate. Most of the propositions advanced in the preceding pages have concerned relationships both within and between these two sets of variables. Since they are the raw materials of any systematic approach to the political party, it would not, perhaps, be amiss to set them down once again.

The main bodies of data on the political party itself have included these:

1. Party structure: the main outlines of party organization; the centralization of power and internal democracy in the party; authority, cohesion, and decision making within the organization.

2. Party functions: the functions of electing, stating issues, and controlling governmental power; style and manner of performing functions; competition with other parties and other political organizations in performing functions.

3. Party clienteles: workers and activists; incentives, rewards, and sanctions; voters and adherents; coalitions of interests and groups; party as a cognitive factor in voting behavior.

4. Parties in systems: the competitive patterns; different structures and functions in major and minor parties; competitive and non-competitive major parties.

This much at least one must know of a political party simply to describe it effectively and fully. For that task, a compilation of the party's wins and losses in elections or of its colorful candidates and personalities will not suffice. Even the most extensive and sophisticated analysis of vote totals and the voting behavior of the American electorate tells us little of the political party as an organization performing specific goal-related tasks in the political system.

The second category of data embraces all of those elements of the political party's environment which shape its organization and its pattern of activities:

1. The political system: the basic processes of policy making and representation; varieties of democracy and their assumptions and corollaries.

2. Non-political institutions and processes: social and economic institutions and processes and their change; basic social composition of the electorate.

3. Political institutions and processes: basic constitutional arrangements and structures; policy-making processes; political parties and political organizations.

4. Regulation of parties and politics: definition of parties and their structure; limits on their activities; definition of membership and control of internal processes; limits on incentives.

5. Election law: the constituency system; systems of representation; registration and ballot form; definition of franchise and electorate; drawing of constituency boundaries; control of candidacy and nomination.

6. Political culture: general patterns of political values, norms, and expectations; general attitudes about politics, government, political parties, and politicians; specific attitudes about party organization and operations.

The relationship between environmental factors and the data on the parties can be represented schematically (Figure 9-1). The pervasive medium of the political environment — from the general political culture and broad social and political institutions to the more specific electoral system and statutory regulation of the parties — shapes the party's recruitment of members and militants, its organizational forms, its intra-party relationships, and its activities and functions.

A simple listing of these categories, however, ignores the problem of their relationships. Ultimately the entire issue of cause in the development of parties, party functions, and party systems can be unraveled only by identifying the direction and priority of the relationships. The political environment shapes primarily the party functions, and those functions — both the immediate task-related functions and the functions the party performs for the broader political system — in turn shape the party organization (Figure 9-2). The existence of a cabinet or presidential system will largely determine what function the party is to perform in organizing power in the legislature; so also will widely held expectations about the proper relationship between the political party and its

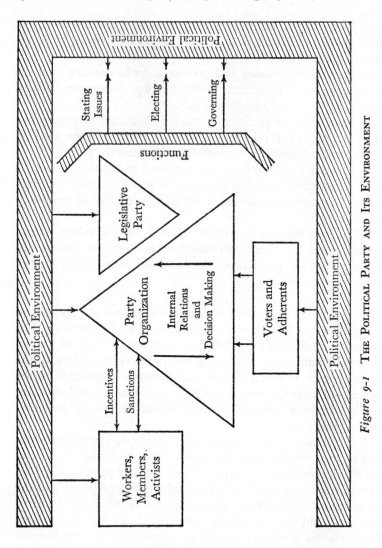

Figure 9-1 THE POLITICAL PARTY AND ITS ENVIRONMENT

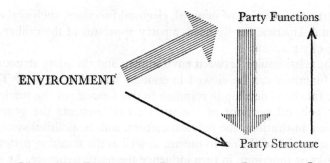

ENVIRONMENT

Party Functions

Party Structure

Figure 9-2 RELATIONSHIP BETWEEN THE PARTY AND ITS ENVIRONMENT

elected representatives. Earlier chapters outlined changes abroad in the American party system today: the decline of the urban machine, the rise of middle-class membership parties, and the party's increasing difficulty in monopolizing its electoral role. All these trends — indeed, any questions of change in a political party or party system — involve exactly these relationships.

Although the main lines of influence run from environment to party function to party structure, the political environment does also secondarily affect organization, and organization in turn limits the functional capabilities of the party. Hence the smaller vectors in Figure 9-2. Cultural values and attitudes toward intra-party democracy or the statutory regulation of the party hierarchy do influence the development of party organization. And a party diminished by popular distrust, by the loss of its most potent rewards, and by crippling regulation will be sharply limited in the functions it can perform and the ways in which it can perform them. It is, of course, arguable that such a relationship exists only in an immediate, proximate sense. Fundamentally the political environment shapes the party functions, and the expectations and statutory regulation of party structure merely reflect those functional demands, needs, and expectations. We are here, however, dealing with proximate cause and influence, and at that level the total political environment shapes party organization as well as party functions. They, in turn, influence each other, even though the main lines of influence run from party functions to structure.

A party organization of minimal, electoral functions, such as those of rural America, hardly needs a party apparatus of the caliber of a big-city machine.

The relationships between environment and the party structure and functions can be viewed in another way (Figure 9-3). The basic functions develop in response to the demands of the particularly political portions of the party's environment: the general political institutions, the political culture, and the political system. These aspects of the environment, as well as the resulting patterns of tasks or functions, in turn influence the party structure. At the same time, the political culture and the non-governmental aspects of the party environment — the social and economic institutions, the composition of the electorate, and the interests and goals of the population — combine to influence the recruitment of party clienteles and the development of other competing political organizations. These clienteles and political organizations then affect party structure and the performance of its functions. One point, however, must be made clear about Figure 9-3. The lines of influence shown are only the chief and dominant ones. Secondary, reinforcing, and reciprocating relationships exist in most cases.

An example may help to clarify Figure 9-3. The reader will notice that the focus of the scheme, the way in which the parties carry out their functions, occupies the center of the diagram. It is also the conceptual center of the scheme, the point at which the sum of influences on the party can best be seen and expressed. The American parties' way of carrying out the function of stating issues and programs is illustrative. That performance is, first of all, determined by the definition, within the context of the political system and political culture, of the American party's responsibilities for program and issue. It may also be limited by the other functions assigned to the party, in this case by the primacy of the incompatible electing function. Party structure — the absence of mass-membership organizations and policy-making organs — further influences the performance of this task. So also do directly influential aspects of the environment such as American federalism and the separation of powers. Similarly, the party's issue concerns will reflect its competition with other parties and with non-party political organizations, such as interest groups, which may also be

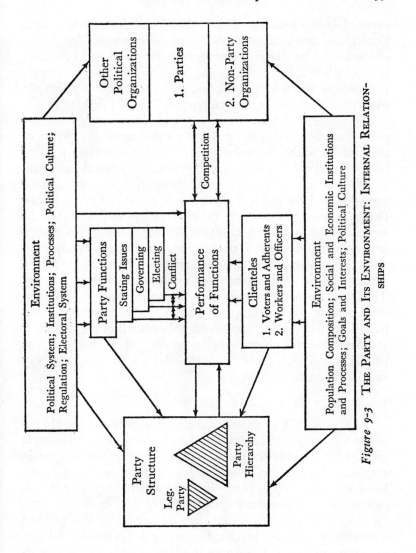

Figure 9-3 THE PARTY AND ITS ENVIRONMENT: INTERNAL RELATIONSHIPS

engaged in the business of spreading ideologies and programs. Finally, the nature of the party's clienteles impinges. The degree of ideological involvement among the party voters and adherents, plus their plural and cross-cutting group loyalties influence performance of this function. So, too, does the extent to which the party's workers seek ideological rewards from political activity.

These general statements of relationship have assumed that the party does not develop in a political vacuum and that it generally must submit to the determinants of the political and non-political processes and cultures outside it. However, the political party may modify that environment. It may, through its own educational activities, alter the political culture, or as an interest group it may change statutory regulations, the electoral system, or even some aspects of the political institutions. Barring its ability to change environmental elements, it may make adaptations and sharply reduce the impact of the environment. Thus have the American parties wriggled out of statutory regulations on their finances. Then, too, the party may also turn aside the pressures of the environment by suppressing them, much as the American parties have diverted pressures for ideological concern into less-popular and less-powerful channels. The building of a theory of the parties, therefore, cannot be premised on a series of one-way causal relationships.

FRAGMENTS OF A PARTY THEORY

A statement of the chief lines of relationship between the party and its environment, however, is only a simple model of the most general relationships and categories involved in a theory of the party. The real job of theorizing involves the identification of specific and continuing relationships among specific components of these categories. We are, in other words, faced with the necessity of showing that specific kinds of political environments produce specific forms of party structure and specific types of function. Since we have been slowly acquiring scattered theoretical propositions of widely accepted validity about the political party, we are not completely without guidelines for a theory of the party. These fragments of party theory do not yet add up to a party theory, but they suggest the direction in which the belated search for that theory can most profitably be directed.

Although the Duverger categories of party organization have occasioned some criticism and reservation, most scholars have agreed on the validity of their main outline. Table 9-1 presents the simplified configurations of the cadre and mass-membership parties to which we referred in Chapter 3. Although few parties may meet all aspects of these two main (and "pure") party types, they do represent main tendencies and directions among the democratic parties.

Table 9-1 COMPARISON OF CADRE AND MASS-MEMBERSHIP POLITICAL PARTIES

	Cadre Parties	Mass-Membership Parties
Structural unit	Limited largely to actives and militants; informal cliques and committees	Large membership; club-like, inclusive, participation style of local organization
Nature of organization	Weakly articulated; unclear lines of authority and relationship; only periodic activity	Fully articulated; full hierarchy with many lines of internal control; year-around activity
Internal distribution of power	Tends to be decentralized; legislative party also autonomous or dominant	Tends to be centralized; national party exerts control over legislative party
Leadership	Leadership of notables, elected officeholders, or social-economic elites	Tends to develop own leadership corps from party militants
Functions	Largely electoral; not ideologically inclined; minimal in function; brokerage party	Both electoral and ideological; maximal in function; tends to be doctrinaire
Relationship to status quo	Centrist; favors status quo	Reformist; seeks change in status quo

These consistent sets of characteristics that mark the cadre and mass-membership parties suggest a linkage of data that can guide the descriptive task. Having identified some of the salient characteristics within a political party, one can reasonably anticipate some of the others. In addition, these sets of characteristics support the theoretical assumptions explained earlier about the relationship between party structure and function. Indeed, they go further than that. They also suggest a high degree of congruence among the four elements of the party: function, structure, clienteles, and performance of the functions. They do not, of course, indicate the cause or priority of causes for it, but the relationship among them is perfectly compatible with the suggested relationships of Figure 9-3.

The typologies of the cadre and mass-membership parties relate to another important element of party theory. Logically, their different patterns of party function and structure ought to reflect differences in the political system, the non-political institutions and processes, and in the political cultures that might account for those differences. Especially, the presence of some of each in one party system would seem to indicate divisions within the political culture, or sharply differing social characteristics, or, possibly, a series of differential demands on political organizations by the political system.

A second and different theoretical approach to the political parties — one that has engaged their students in rounds and rounds of controversy — concerns the explanation of the party system. That problem we have discussed at length in the second chapter. Basically, the party system reflects the consensus and diversity of the society. Then, political culture, specific political institutions, and electoral law exert reinforcing pressures on it. But the force of the general political system and other basic social institutions and values predominate. Similarly, within various areas of a single political system such as the American, the pattern of two-party competition depends on social heterogeneity. The move to two-party politics in many parts of the United States has resulted from the diversification of interests and life in those areas. In these cases, too, institutional factors hold fairly constant. Again, theoretical speculation in this area suggests the primacy over the parties of basic political and non-political environmental factors, rather than electoral law and statutory regulation.

Third, one can see developing an area of theory about the political parties as organizations. In Chapter 5 we explored one aspect of that organizational system: the pattern of incentives and rewards with which the party attracts and controls its activists. Studies of democracy and decision making within the party, from Michels to the present, deal with another aspect of the party as an organization. Finally, we have suggested another facet of the question in discussing the functional uses and implications of convention and primary nominations for the American parties. But, again, these are fragments. The growing literature on large organizations, already highly developed in the areas of social and economic organization, has yet to be applied to the American political organizations. We have yet to discuss systematically the problems of cohesion and conflict, the authority relationships, and the goal-attaining or goal-satisfying behavior of the political party.

These three illustrative beginnings of theoretical development in the study of political parties indicate that it may be useful to divide the total theoretical problem into three subdivisions.

1. The first of these theoretical sub-areas would concern the theory of specific types of party structure and function. Under what circumstances does a party system shift from cadre parties to those of a broader membership base? What implications have specific organizational forms for the specific activities of the party? What, indeed, are the impacts on parties of particular political institutions, electoral systems, or political cultures? To take an illustration from the realities of local American politics, what effects does non-partisanship have on the local parties? These theoretical questions — which include those of the Duverger categories — would attempt, in other words, to explain the nature of the parties and their variation among political systems and within a single system.

2. The second area of theory is that concerned with the party's internal organizational affairs: its need to attract workers, to maintain internal cohesion and stability, and to achieve organizational goals. Much of the study of patronage and other incentives suggests this type of theory. How does a political party use and manipulate its reward system to achieve the goals of the party? What factors determine the patterns of authority and decision making

within the political party? What systems and mechanisms has the party for selecting its leadership? This sub-area of theory would embrace all the considerations of organizational theory and apply it to the party. It would also include the theoretical propositions about individual behavior in the party organization — what attracts participation by workers, what holds them, what accounts for differences, stability, and change in activity.

3. Finally, we are concerned with theory that deals with the relationships between and among parties in the party system, and then, between the parties and other political organizations competing with them in the performance of the political functions. The quest for a theory of the party system is typified by the attempts to explain the special case of the two-party system. Related is the question of the determinants of different patterns of competition within one-party systems, a question one might call that of the relationship between the party system and its sub-systems. Finally, this area of theory might well, as we have suggested earlier, develop types of systems that would explain the total division of labor and the total patterns of competition in political function among all the political organizations of a political system — interest groups, factions, power elites, and personal followings, as well as political parties.

PARTIES IN THE POLITICAL SYSTEM

The recent pioneering work of Almond and Coleman, *The Politics of the Developing Areas*, proposes a set of four political functions that must by definition be performed in every political system. Their names are reasonably self-explanatory: political socialization and recruitment, interest articulation, interest aggregation (*i.e.*, organization and combination), and political communication. In the performance of these broad functions in the political system, the roles of the parties vary. Those of the older Western democracies perform largely the function of interest aggregation, the combining of groups and interests into larger aggregates of political power. The parties of the developing areas, however, may perform most or all of the other functions. For example, in the absence of formal interest groups they articulate specific interests, or they absorb the interest groups as auxiliary party organs. Western parties, in other words, clearly share the performance of these four political functions with interest groups, mass media, primary social groups, informal community elites, and personal cliques and factions.

In this essay we have employed a set of three functions — electing, propagandizing, and governing — drawn not from the demands of the total political system but from the practice of democratic parties and from the specific demands of political institutions. These functions are directly related to the political process as the overt and "manifest" political tasks the party performs. As manifest functions they are also "functional" for the parties in that their goals and rewards — as parties and as politically active individuals — can only be achieved through their successful performance. And yet there is no reason to view these functions as the everlasting property of parties in general or of any particular political party. In fact, in the American system it seems that for the present at least the parties are finding it increasingly difficult to hold their present position in the performance of the classic party functions. They no longer control the major share of political expertise and political loyalties they once did.

In this sense the political parties operate as political "means," *Conclusion* and their tasks and functions find meaning only within the institutions, expectations, and interests they serve. We cannot, therefore, decide issues of the "proper" functions for the political parties in the abstract and apart from their political environment. One can hardly condemn the French parties for failing to achieve the legislative discipline and cohesion that the British institutions and political processes demand. One can also assess a political party according to the expectations of the political culture. Quite apart from the successes and failures the American city machines may have had, it is incontestable that they frequently outraged the ethical standards and political values of a large number of their constituents, though not perhaps so large a number as we would like to imagine.

To return to functional categories similar to those of the Almond and Coleman study, one can say that the political parties perform another set of functions for the political system as a whole. They reduce effectively the number of political options to

manageable numbers, bring order and focus to the political struggle, simplify issues and frame alternatives, compromise conflicting
interests, recruit political leadership, personalize and dramatize
politics, stabilize political debate and allegiances, and enhance the
political power of the "insignificant" individual. These are the
latent, more remote functions the parties perform. They are
"functional" not for the parties themselves, but for the political
system as a whole. That is, their effective performance contributes
to the goals and well-being of the total political system. But again
one should be clear that although the political system may require the performance of these functions, it does not require that
the political party perform them. The only relevant question is
whether or not the parties can perform them more effectively than
other types of political organization.

The question of party effectiveness and performance, then,
comes down to its relative efficiency in performing these two
levels of function. The case for the primacy of the party on both
of these functional levels rests on the party's basic and distinguishing characteristics: its exclusively political nature, its dominance
of the electoral processes, and its stable and inclusive organization.
The parties, therefore, are more open in their operations, more
receptive to new personnel and interests, better able to symbolize
programs and choices, and more liable to public judgment on past
performance. Thus they can more effectively contest elections and
organize governmental power, just as they can simultaneously perform the integrative functions for the political system more satisfactorily than the other political organizations. The personal
clique, the interest group, the economic or social elite, the faction,
and the other political organizations lack the stability and durabil-
ity to provide lasting guidelines for the political process. Their
narrow base affords a restricted ground on which to recruit leadership or settle differences. They proliferate political choices instead of reducing them. And they deal in political isolates rather
than political aggregates, in difference rather than consensus.

When the political parties lose their chief characteristics as political parties, they, too, lose their effectiveness. Key's study of the
loose factions within the dominant parties of the American Southern states indicates that they cannot make these contributions to

the democratic system as satisfactorily as the stable party can. And one can wonder similarly how effective as organizing foci may be the African parties that regroup and realign every few years, or the French legislative groups that form and reform as free and shifting alliances of parties and personal followings.

PARTY REFORM AND REALISM

We have spoken earlier about the tendency to treat the parties as freely formed political organizations, independent of the political environment around them and subject only to the limits of willpower and personal effort. The political party has come in the American political culture to have an unreal life as a prime mover in the political system, as a freely adaptable, all-purpose instrument of political reform and change. The lack of a theory of the political party has, in other words, taken its toll in naive and indefensible assumptions about the party.

Probably because of its instrumental and informal nature, the political party seems a likely tool of reform. Though the institutions and structures of government may be outlined and set down in law and constitution, those of the party rarely are. They seem, consequently, more ephemeral and susceptible of change than the more firmly fixed and established legislatures and executives. Furthermore, the party is the dynamic agent in the political system, an organization associated much more with action and movement, with the dynamics of human behavior and processes, than are the more stolid political institutions. As the classic political instruments they are well-suited to be the protagonists of changes. The report of the committee of the American Political Science Association clearly views the party as such an instrument of reform, as an avenging angel, through which broader ideological and political goals, especially those associated with a particular concept of democracy, can be achieved.

The reformism so often imposed on the political parties — whether it aims to reform the parties themselves or to use them as agents of broader political reform — overlooks how intricately the parties are enmeshed in the restraints and bonds of the outside environment. The authors of *Toward a More Responsible Two-Party System*, in fact, devote little attention to the practicability and possibility of achieving its myriad prescriptions. The parties they describe seem curiously abstracted from the American society and political traditions. American state legislatures make the same mistake. They seem to assume that they can, by waving the legislative wand, alter and shape the party at will. The political pros, also, fall into the same fallacies as the reformers. They often subscribe to an ideal of party organization, which they take as the panacea for all the ills and failings of the party. Should the party lose an election, the remedy is always "better organization."

For all those who so overlook the multiplicity of the causes and pressures at work on the parties, the disappointments are many. The reforms of the reformers do not endure, and the prescriptions of the American Political Science Association committee have not even pitted the stony resistance of the parties. Indeed, a good share of the cynicism with which so many men of good will view the parties may be a result of these unreal hopes and illusions. The parties are, as are all social institutions, deeply conservative organizations, rooted in political cultures, conventions, and other institutions. They will not and cannot be easily displaced or easily altered without altering some or all of their environment.

In the long run, changes within the political parties have come as the result of changes in their political surroundings. As electorates expand, as political cultures change, as the patterns of incentives shift — as all these factors change, the parties do also in order to adapt to them. Since the governmental environment of the parties generally remains more fixed than the non-governmental, these changes reflect more easily the shifts in the non-governmental: in population composition, in standards of living, in levels of literacy and education, in technological advances, in general attitudes and political culture, and even in expectations about democracy. Indeed, it is a continuing problem for the parties that the governmental environment often fastens on the party — through fixed legal forms, regulations, and controls — an aspect of its environment that frequently does not keep abreast of basic changes in the non-governmental aspects of the political system.

When major change and reform occur within the political parties, they most often take place as a response to the changing environmental circumstances. The changes planned and engineered by men, in other words, take place within the fact of a "ripeness" of more basic influences. To this extent the recent revolt and successes of the new American urban reformers against the entrenched city machines succeed because the incentives, the political culture, and the political services supporting it had, to a considerable extent, already eroded. The city machines were and are ripe for the plucking in many American cities.

Slow and resistant to change though they are, the parties are in the aggregate no more and no less flexible than the other political institutions. Much of their value, indeed, arises from their institutionalized stability. They cannot single-handedly reform the political system and political institutions, but that is not their job. They are unplanned instruments by which democratic majorities amass and effect their political power. Except to a small group of admirers who consider them as ends in themselves — and as esthetically pleasing political artifacts — they are means by which we promote and facilitate the systems of representation and decision making in a democracy. They are not, however, the key to that system. The maze of political influences, causes, and needs underlying the political system may have a point of origin, but it is not in the parties. The value of their role in the political system is secure without that claim.

APPENDIX

The study of American political parties

I. THE SCHOLARLY DEVELOPMENT

The study of political parties in American political science has over the last 50 years been marked by an impressive freedom and variety of approach. A good deal of its history, however, can be traced in the five main traditions that have dominated its scholarship and colored its achievements: historicism, the voting studies, reformism, activism, and political reporting.

The tradition of historicism is an old and honorable one in the study of political parties, and many of its products — Wilfred Binkley's *American Political Parties* (New York: A. A. Knopf, 1962), for example — have been valuable additions to the literature on American parties. Most of the party histories, however, have in reality been histories of Presidential elections and candidates, four-year by four-year surveys of shifts in the national coalitions of the parties, as well as accounts of the nominating conventions and Presidential campaigns. When they have dealt with shorter periods, they have often focused on ideological movements and colorful leaders — an emphasis apparent in the preference of the party historians for the minor parties over the two major parties. But with few exceptions, such as William N. Chambers' *Political Parties in a New Nation* (New York: Oxford University Press, 1963), they do not concern themselves with the vastly more complicated and obscure history of the parties as political organizations. They say little of party structure, relationships within the parties, party personnel and leadership, or the ways in which parties contest elections and organize political power. And the attention given the third parties to the almost total neglect of the major parties almost seems to indicate that the canons of relevance and importance have given way to a fascination with the quaint and bizarre in American politics.

Within the last thirty years the second tradition, that of the election and voting studies, has entered the mainstream of scholarship on the parties. The use first of aggregate vote totals and now of the data from sample surveys has produced a welter of works that have studied chiefly the parties' electorates. In the 1930's and 1940's these studies were typified by Arthur Holcombe's works based on the analysis of gross election results (for example, his *The New Party Politics* [New York: Norton, 1933]). From the data on which his and similar studies rested, generalization was possible only in aggregates, and the political analysis they produced tended to sectional, regional, or urban-rural interpretations of shifting party electorates. More recently the work of Lazarsfeld, Berelson, and the Survey Research Center of the University of Michigan, especially the latter's *The American Voter* (New York: Wiley, 1960), dominate this genre. These men have claimed no more for their work than that it deals with electoral behavior; the SRC, in fact, has explicitly noted that the political party appears in its work only as a perception by its supporters. Nonetheless, the voting studies have tended in less cautious circles — as the party histories did before them — to obscure the distinction between the political party and its electorate. For skeletal parties such as the American ones, the party's electorate is, however, almost totally independent of the party as a political organization.

Third, there has always been with the study of American parties a reformist, even a muckraking tradition. This tradition led scholars of the parties to support the direct primary, non-partisan elections, regulations of party finance and party organization, and attempts to make the parties more ideological and "responsible." And because the old urban machine was the focus of their reforming, it led them to scores of studies on Tammany Hall, assorted bosses from Tweed and Penrose to Hague and Curley, the political clubs and machines themselves, and on the personalities and rascalities of their operations. The best of these studies are landmarks — Harold Gosnell's *Machine Politics: Chicago Model* (Chicago: University of Chicago Press, 1937), for instance — for they directed the study of politics to a new and more extensive field observation and to more rigorous analytical techniques. But others were more outraged than analytical, more in the tradition of Lincoln Steffens than of empirical social science. Since these studies were almost the only ones of their time that dealt with the party as an organization, a great imbalance in the study of the American parties resulted. For all the effort spent on these political feudalities and their lords and barons, there was no counterbalancing study of the less dramatic and more typical small city and rural parties, and no real studies of state or national parties, either.

More recently a tradition of activism has developed in the study of parties, one that seems in many quarters to suggest that doing is more fruitful than studying, that there is some knowledge about parties and politics that cannot be transmitted through the printed page. This tradition has taken teachers and their students into the field to observe political conventions and other party activity, to join parties and share in the work of the ward and precinct, and to seek the practical wisdom of the political practitioner. Regardless of its advantages in interest and in recruiting new personnel for the parties, such activism has often been substituted for the scholarly goals and the scholarly experience. In its emphasis on activity and on the specific event and the first-hand data, it works against the development of scholarly propositions and theory.

Finally, we have a tradition of what is at best a political journalism and at worst a political inside-dopesterism. Along with the tradition of activism it probably works against the development of a body of scholarly knowledge; taken together, the two explain in part the non-theoretical orientation of the study of American parties. This journalistic tradition revels in saucy and salty political anecdotes, reporting colorful events and personalities, retailing the latest political gossip and speculation, and exploring the "inside story." The emphasis is on individual personalities, immediate events and strategies, and the Byzantine convolutions and practices of the more devious political artists. Indeed, one can argue that this level of analysis, in that it deals with personal causes and discrete events, is really no analysis at all. At the very most it is analysis of contemporary events and behavior in the manner of the most skillful political journalists.

These traditions by no means account for all that has been done in the name of scholarship in political parties over the past 50 years. One cannot fit into these traditions the studies of the relationship between the American parties and the American political system — for example, the informal debate between Herring and Schattschneider over the place of the party in American democracy. Nor do these categories accommodate a seminal work such as V. O. Key's *Southern Politics* (New York: A. A. Knopf, 1949), possibly the single most influential and valuable work of the postwar period on the American parties. Nor does this list include an old and declining tradition: the study of interest groups within the field of political parties. No doubt that study was often afflicted with a muckraking tone, but the large and powerful groups now languish as an unexplored area of political science.

Despite these notable exceptions, the five traditions have dominated the American study of political parties and have shaped its products and fruits. When added together, they have unhappily left American political science short of a description of the American parties and their operations. An impressive effort by two generations of scholarship on the American parties has failed, above all, to develop a theory of the political party — a theory about its relationship to the political system and other aspects of its environment, or a theory about its structure and function, or its position in a party system. None of the five dominant traditions directed political scientists to questions of the party as a political organization with important functions in a broader political system. From 1900 to 1945 the study of political parties shared with the rest of political science a preference for "hard-headed," practical description and activism and a suspicion of theoretical propositions.

Closely related to this failure to begin the task of theorizing has been a predominantly non-organizational view of the political parties in these five traditions. Too infrequently have they separated the party as a political organization from the party's electoral coalition. There is missing a clear and firm definition of the political party as one of a number of types of political organization that perform specific tasks in specific ways in the political system. And when scholarship has turned to the parties as political organizations it has been to the atypical, colorful, even outrageous political bosses and machines to the neglect of other party types. The consequences have been twofold. This distorted description of the party organization has found its way into the public image of the parties, giving an impression of the parties far less than accurate. It has contributed to a devil theory of American politics that finds a boss in every ward and a machine in every county. Furthermore, it has encouraged scholars of the parties to take at face value the statutory hierarchies the states create for the parties and to assume that full and functioning party organizations exist in every electoral district in the country.

The first fifty or sixty years of the study of American political parties have not, of course, been without achievements. Large numbers of excellent studies, many of which are noted in the following section, have made the American parties and party system the most extensively described in the world. Furthermore, that scholarship has had beneficial results apart from the substance of the subject itself. Scholars of the parties have been among the leaders in a battle to overthrow the institutional and legal orientations that dominated American political science until the second World War. They rescued the informal political processes and the political behavior within formal structures from an unfortunate obscurity, and they were among the first to expand and refine the empirical methods and newer statistical analysis that American political science now takes for granted. In addition, much of the work on the parties and party systems of other countries owes its inspiration to American scholarship. Many of the leading works on the party systems of a number of other countries are by American scholars or by other scholars trained in the American traditions. The development of a comparative study of political parties, therefore, owes much to the traditions of the American study of parties.

The unfinished business and scholarly needs of the study of American parties have been suggested throughout this essay; they are also present by implication in the description of the main traditions of the study in the past. It remains only to sum them up briefly here.

American scholars of the parties, first of all, have to fill lacunae in their description of the American parties. The following survey of the leading sources indicates the absence of materials on the organization and operations of the American parties as political organizations. As a rough index to the problem, one might say that the voids will not be filled until we know at least as much about the parties as we know of their electorates, as much about rural and small-town parties as about their metropolitan counterparts, as much about other party functions as about their campaigning for election, and as much about their leaders and workers as about their more casual voters.

We have also been slow to clarify the concepts central to the study of political parties. The necessary clarification might well begin with the party itself, for the stories of Presidential candidates, the platforms and issues, the rigors of the campaign trail, or even intensive analyses of election results relate only indirectly to the party as a political organization. Subsidiary concepts have suffered the same neglect. Competitiveness in elections is the single criterion by which we define party systems, but there is little agreement on a definition of competition. The concept of "faction" remains as obscure, and we have no consensus on an operational definition for determining factionalism in a party. And, to take a final example, what measures have we of party organizational strength other than its capacity to win elections? On these and many other matters of concept and definition the need is clear for serious thought.

Third, there are abundant signs that the American study of political parties needs new data on which to work. The easy availability of electoral and voting data has undoubtedly led to their overuse and exhaustion, even by new and more sophisticated techniques of analysis. To open new areas of data about the party, its operations and functions, its personnel and leadership, its relationship to other political institutions, its competition with other parties and political organizations requires a greater dependence on field observation, participation, and interviewing. Political scientists have almost exhausted the documentary data on parties and politics; the census data, the yearbooks, the election reports, and the newspaper files have yielded all they have. The new data on party recruitment of candidates, endorsements in primaries, authority relationships within the party, and modes of organization — to take a few examples — must be gathered from local informants and observers in tiring, costly, often dispiriting, and even unreliable field work. The only alternative may well be more and more intensive analysis of old data, probably passing the point of diminishing returns.

Finally, scholarship on the American parties, unless it is to fall behind in the concerns of the rest of American political science, must press its search for more middle-range theory of the political party. Increasingly it appears that it needs that enrichment of theory if only for its own guidance in seeking relevant questions to explore and in developing new bodies of data about the American parties. The expansion of the comparative study of political parties needs it even more desperately as a framework of comparative analysis. In the search for theories of the parties the lead has been taken, not by an American, but by the French scholar Maurice Duverger, in his *Political Parties* (New York: Wiley, 1954). Although criticism of Duverger's naïveté about the American parties and of his monistic theory of party development has been fairly common, few American scholars have taken up the challenge of proposing alternative explanations. Surprisingly, in view of political science's recent eclecticism, they have been unwilling to borrow from the concepts, models, and theories of the related social sciences. It was suggested earlier in this essay, for instance, that the entire body of knowledge about large-scale organizations now being developed throughout the social sciences is relevant to the study of American parties.

II. SOURCES AND BIBLIOGRAPHY

The standard texts now in service in American colleges and universities have been the main integrating works on the American parties. Of those, V. O. Key's *Politics, Parties, and Pressure Groups*, 4th edition (New York: Thos. Y. Crowell, 1958) is the most comprehensive and authoritative. It goes beyond the usual scope of a text, introducing new and original analysis, and it surely deserves its status as the standard treatise on the subject. Then, too, Austin Ranney and Willmoore Kendall's *Democracy and the American Party System* (New York: Harcourt, Brace and Co., 1956), aside from its excellent survey of pertinent literature, relates the parties to the broader context of the democratic political system and to a democratic ideology. It also contains useful and unusual chapters on institutional and intellectual histories of the political parties.

E. E. Schattschneider's *Party Government* (New York: Rinehart and Co., 1942) is a shorter, classic, analytical essay on the American parties. It presents a viewpoint critical of the parties' decentralization and weakness. Wilfred Binkley's *American Political Parties*, 4th edition (New York: A. A. Knopf, 1962) offers the standard, compact history of the national party elections and electoral coalitions. For a stimulating account of the origins of the American parties, see William N. Chambers, *Political Parties in a New Nation* (New York: Oxford University Press, 1963). For suggestions of recent developments in the American parties, the reader might also see Schattschneider's *The Semi-Sovereign People* (New York: Holt, Rinehart and Winston, 1960); James M. Burns' *Deadlock of Democracy* (Englewood Cliffs, N.J.: Prentice-Hall, 1963), and Stephen K. Bailey, *The Condition of Our National Political Parties* (Fund for the Republic, 1959).

The most comprehensive comparative analysis of the parties of the Western democracies remains Maurice Duverger's *Political Parties* (New York: John Wiley and Sons, 1954). It propounds a monistic causal theory in which the electoral system explains far too much about the parties and party systems. Nonetheless, it contains a vast amount of comparative material and a number of valid and useful insights and categories. It has also been the most influential of the comparative studies, and it pushes closer than any of its competitors to a theory of political parties. Sigmund Neumann has edited *Modern Political Parties* (Chicago: University of Chicago Press, 1956), a volume of essays by distinguished American scholars on the party systems of Britain, the Commonwealth, France, Belgium, Scandinavia, the United States, the Soviet Union, the Soviet satellites, Japan, and Western Germany. Only Neumann's concluding essay, however, can be said to be comparative.

Of the party systems in the rest of the world, that of Great Britain has been blessed with most ample and successful literature on the parties. Robert McKenzie's *British Political Parties* (New York: St. Martin's Press, 1955) remains the best work on the subject. Its scope and coverage is not as broad as Key's for the American parties, but it has the advantage of an organizing focus: the distribution of power and authority within the major British parties. Phillip Williams, in *Politics in Post-War France* (London: Longmans, Green, 1954), deals with the period up to 1954 and relates the parties to the political system of the Republic. Myron Weiner's *Party Politics in India* (Princeton: Princeton University Press, 1957), however, focuses chiefly on the development of the parties and of factionalism within them. The study of *African Political Parties* by Thomas Hodgkin (Penguin Books, 1961) succinctly conquers the complexity of its subject.

For lengthier bibliographies, the reader might consult the bibliographical essay in Neumann's *Modern Political Parties*. Excellent also are the cumulative footnotes of the Key and Ranney-Kendall texts on the American parties.

CHAPTER I. THE POLITICAL PARTY

For general material on the political party, four works already mentioned should be recommended again: Duverger's *Political Parties*, Schattschneider's *Party Government*, the Chambers history, and the final essay in Neumann's *Modern Political Parties*. A challenging and useful essay on the study of American parties is Neil McDonald's *The Study of Political Parties* (Garden City, N.Y.: Doubleday and Co., 1955). The same is also true of Avery Leiserson's *Parties and Politics* (New York: A. A. Knopf, 1958).

p. 7   The two questions on identifiers come, respectively, from the Survey Research Center's questionnaire (see Campbell, *et al.*, *The American Voter*) and from the Minnesota Poll of the Minneapolis *Star* and *Tribune*.

p. 11   Chambers, *Political Parties in a New Nation*, p. 111.

CHAPTER 2.   PARTIES IN SYSTEMS

Book II of Duverger remains the most thorough exploration of the party systems. V. O. Key's *Southern Politics* (New York: A. A. Knopf, 1949) can be taken as an extensive and excellent case study of a one-party system. It may also be the finest field study on the American parties of the past generation. Similarly useful are the regional studies of American parties and politics such as Duane Lockard's *New England State Politics* (Princeton: Princeton University Press, 1959).

p. 18   For an imaginative attack on the problem of competitiveness, see Joseph Schlesinger, "A Two-Dimensional Scheme for Classifying the States According to Degree of Inter-Party Competition," *American Political Science Review*, XLIX (1955), pp. 1120-1128.

p. 22   The data on American party systems comes from Ranney and Kendall, *Democracy and the American Party System*, pp. 161-164.

p. 25   Key, *Southern Politics*, p. 52.

p. 27   For theories of the party system see Schattschneider, *Party Government*, and Duverger; also relevant and illustrative are Leslie Lipson, "The Two-Party System in British Politics," *American Political Science Review*, XLVII (1953), pp. 337-358; and James C. Charlesworth, "Is Our Party System Natural," *Annals*, vol. CCLIX (1948), pp. 1-9.

p. 32   See, for instance, Robert Golembiewski, "A Taxonomic Approach to State Political Party Strength," *Western Political Quarterly*, XI (1958), pp. 494-513.

CHAPTER 3.   THE ORGANIZATION: FORM AND CONTROL

Again, reference must be made to Duverger, Book I, to McKenzie on the British parties, and to Key and the other texts for materials on the American parties. Perhaps the only substantial body of description on the American parties as organizations has been that on the American urban machine. Harold Gosnell's *Machine Politics: Chicago Model* (Chicago: University of Chicago Press, 1937) represents the genre well. More recently, James Q. Wilson has described the new club movement very well in his *The Amateur Democrat* (Chicago: University of Chicago Press, 1962).

p. 39 From a paper delivered by Marvin Harder and Thomas Ungs at the May, 1963, meetings of the Midwest Conference of Political Scientists at Chicago, Illinois.

p. 39 Schattschneider, *Party Government*, p. 129.

p. 41 McKenzie, *British Political Parties*, p. 55.

p. 47 For variants in American party organization, see Frank J. Sorauf, "Extra-Legal Political Parties in Wisconsin," *American Political Science Review*, XLVIII (1954), pp. 692-704; and Currin V. Shields, "A Note on Party Organization: The Democrats in California," *Western Political Quarterly*, VII (1954), pp. 673-683.

p. 49 Robert Michels, *Political Parties* (Glencoe: The Free Press, 1949).

p. 49 For a perceptive critique of Michels, see C. W. Cassinelli, "The Law of Oligarchy," *American Political Science Review*, XLVII (1953), pp. 773-784. Two notable studies of the interest group using the Michels thesis are: Oliver Garceau, *The Political Life of the American Medical Association* (Cambridge: Harvard University Press, 1941) and Seymour M. Lipset, *et al.*, *Union Democracy* (Glencoe: The Free Press, 1956).

p. 55 James M. Burns, *Deadlock of Democracy*, p. 236.

p. 55 See Julian Woodward and Elmo Roper, "Political Activity of American Citizens," *American Political Science Review*, XLIV (1950), pp. 872-885.

p. 57 Wilson, *The Amateur Democrat*.

CHAPTER 4. ISSUES AND IDEOLOGY

Party platforms, credos, and manifestos, along with other expressions of individual ideologies, offer primary material on this aspect of party life. Kirk Porter and Donald B. Johnson, in *National Party Platforms, 1840-1956* (Urbana: University of Illinois Press, 1956), have collected relevant American documents. More occasional works such as campaign biographies, memoirs, party histories, and personal declarations are also valuable. Seymour Harris's recent work on the economic ideology of the American parties, *The Economics of the Political Parties* (New York: Macmillan & Co., 1962) indicates fruitful directions for future work. Two excellent summaries on this topic, drawn largely from the voting studies, are: Seymour M. Lipset, *Political Man* (Garden City, N.Y.: Doubleday and Co., 1960) and V. O. Key, *Public Opinion and American Democracy* (New York: A. A. Knopf, 1961).

p. 64   James M. Burns, *The Deadlock of Democracy*, p. 208.
p. 64   For an analysis of the political effects of the pluralistic American society, see Schattschneider, *Party Government*, and Arthur N. Holcombe, *Our More Perfect Union* (Cambridge: Harvard University Press, 1950).
p. 70   See Herbert McCloskey, *et al.*, "Issue Conflict and Consensus in American Party Leaders and Followers, *American Political Science Review*, LIV (1960), pp. 406-427.
p. 76   The reference to President Eisenhower comes from Sherman Adams, *Firsthand Report* (New York: Harper and Bros., 1961).

CHAPTER 5.   THE STRUCTURE OF INCENTIVES

Little has, unfortunately, been written on the party as an organization. Yet, the treatises on organization theory provide a wealth of suggestions. See especially James March and Herbert Simon, *Organizations* (New York: John Wiley and Sons, 1958) and Amitai Etzioni, *A Comparative Analysis of Complex Organizations* (Glencoe: The Free Press, 1961). Stimson Bullitt, in his perceptive, if labyrinthine, *To Be a Politician* (Garden City, N.Y.: Doubleday and Co., 1961) examines the rewards of politics far more thoroughly than usual. Studies of the urban machine and patronage do so, too; see especially, James Reichley, *The Art of*

Government: Reform and Organization Politics in Philadelphia
(Fund for the Republic, 1959).

p. 82 I have dealt with patronage uses and rewards in "State
Patronage in a Rural County," *American Political Science Review*, L (1956), pp. 1046-1056.

p. 84 Frank R. Kent, *The Great Game of Politics* (Garden City,
N.Y.: Doubleday, Page, and Co., 1923).

p. 84 Harold Lasswell, *Power and Personality* (New York:
W. W. Norton, 1948).

p. 85 John Fisher, "Please Don't Bite the Politicians," *Harpers*,
CCXXI (Nov., 1960), p. 16.

p. 86 Peter Clark and James Q. Wilson, "Incentive Systems: A
Theory of Organizations," *Administrative Science Quarterly*,
VI (1961), pp. 129-166.

p. 92 March and Simon, *Organizations*, pp. 65-66.

p. 94 Bullitt, *To Be a Politician*, p. 22.

CHAPTER 6. THE CONTEST FOR OFFICE

Here the writings on the American parties are the most complete. Most of the histories, such as Binkley's, focus on the party
in the electoral process. The chief studies of voting behavior also
have elaborated on elections from the viewpoint of the individual
voter and his decisions and perceptions. See Paul Lazarsfeld *et al.*,
The People's Choice, second edition (New York: Columbia University Press, 1948); Bernard Berelson *et al.*, *Voting* (Chicago:
University of Chicago Press, 1954); Angus Campbell *et al.*, *The
Voter Decides* (Evanston: Row, Peterson Co., 1954), and the
already mentioned *American Voter* (New York: John Wiley and
Sons, 1960). Then, too, journalistic studies have had their value
in this area. Samuel Lubell's *Future of American Politics*, second
edition (Garden City, N.Y.: Doubleday and Co., 1956) and Theo-
dore White's *The Making of the President: 1960* (New York:
Atheneum, 1961) are two of the best recent examples. For a full
study of presidential nominating politics at the conventions, see
also Paul David, *et al.*, *The Politics of National Party Conventions* (Washington: The Brookings Institution, 1960). V. O. Key's

American State Politics (New York: A. A. Knopf, 1956) has been a stimulus to a series of studies on the state parties as nominators and electors; these would include Leon D. Epstein, *Politics in Wisconsin* (Madison: University of Wisconsin Press, 1958) and Frank J. Sorauf, *Party and Representation* (New York: Atherton Press, 1963). Other notable works related to the parties as nominators and electors are Stanley Kelley's *Professional Public Relations and Political Power* (Baltimore: Johns Hopkins University Press, 1956) and Alexander Heard's *The Costs of Democracy* (Chapel Hill: University of North Carolina Press, 1960).

p. 98   see William H. Hessler, "Taft Versus Kennedy in Ohio," *The Reporter* (Oct. 25, 1962), pp. 40-42.

p. 107   Key, *American State Politics.*

pp. 111-112   *The American Voter*, mentioned above. The 1952 reference is to *The Voter Decides*, also mentioned above.

p. 113   *The American Voter*, pp. 136-137.

CHAPTER 7.   PARTY AND THE USES OF POWER

Almost all of the writing on the American parties and the uses of governmental power concerns the parties in the legislature. Specialized studies of party and legislative voting include Julius Turner, *Party and Constituency* (Baltimore: Johns Hopkins University Press, 1952) and David B. Truman, *The Congressional Party* (New York: John Wiley and Sons, 1959). For a fuller treatment of party in the lives of legislators see John Wahlke and his associates, *The Legislative System* (New York: John Wiley and Sons, 1962). Burns in *The Deadlock of Democracy* examines in detail the division between legislative and executive parties. For party in the executive one must resort to the general works on the governor and the President (such as those by Clinton Rossiter and Richard Neustadt), as well as biographies and memoirs. For the debate over "party responsibility," the two leading protagonists are E. Pendleton Herring, *The Politics of Democracy* (New York: W. W. Norton, 1940) and Schattschneider, *Party Government* (New York: Rinehart and Co., 1942). The report of the Committee on Political Parties of the American Political Science Association was published as *Toward a More Responsible Two-Party System* (New York: Rinehart and Co., 1950). Criticisms of the report dotted the journals of political science for the next two years, joining and spurring a debate of exceptionally high quality.

p. 116 The first paragraph is drawn from McKenzie, *British Political Parties*, pp. 330-331.

p. 123 On parties and the judiciary see Stuart Nagel, "Political Party Affiliation and Judges' Decisions," *American Political Science Review*, LV (1961), pp. 843-850.

p. 128 Ranney and Kendall, *Democracy and the American Party System*, p. 397.

p. 132 Studies of party cohesion in legislatures include: William Keefe, "Parties, Partisanship, and Public Policy in the Pennsylvania Legislature," *American Political Science Review*, XLVIII (1954), pp. 450-468; Duane Lockard, "Legislative Politics in Connecticut," *American Political Science Review*, XLVIII (1954), pp. 166-173; and Duncan MacRae, "The Relation Between Roll Call Votes and Constituencies in the Massachusetts House of Representatives," *American Political Science Review*, XLVI (1952), pp. 1046-1055.

CHAPTER 8. THE PARTY AND ITS ENVIRONMENT

It is difficult to suggest specific works that deal with these matters; all works on the political parties do to some extent. Duverger discusses the impact of the electoral environment at great length.

p. 144 For a study on districting, see Malcolm Jewell (ed.), *Politics of Reapportionment* (New York: Atherton Press, 1962).

p. 145 A classic work on the relationship between party and the electoral system is Ferdinand Hermens, *Democracy or Anarchy?* (Notre Dame: The Review of Politics, 1941).

p. 148 Robert Wood, *Suburbia* (Boston: Houghton Mifflin, 1958), pp. 155-156.

p. 148 The reference is to David Riesman, *The Lonely Crowd* (Garden City, N.Y.: Doubleday and Co., 1953).

CHAPTER 9.   TOWARD A THEORY OF THE POLITICAL PARTY

Again, little of a general nature seems relevant aside from the Duverger, Neumann, McDonald, and Leiserson books mentioned in the first two paragraphs of this bibliographical note.

p. 164   Gabriel Almond and James Coleman, *The Politics of Developing Areas* (Princeton: Princeton University Press, 1960).

Index